WHO'S YOUR DADDY?

AND OTHER STORIES

ALSO BY GEOFFREY PHILP

Fiction

Uncle Obadiah and the Alien and Other Stories (1997)
Benjamin, My Son (2003)

Poetry

Exodus (1991)
Florida Bound (1995)
Hurricane Center (1998)
Xango Music (2001)
Twelve Poems and a Story for Christmas (2005)

Children's Books

Grandpa Sydney's Anancy Stories (2007)

WHO'S YOUR DADDY?

AND OTHER STORIES

GEOFFREY PHILP

PEEPAL TREE

First published in Great Britain in 2009
Peepal Tree Press Ltd
17 King's Avenue
Leeds LS6 1QS
England

ISBN13: 9781845230777

ARTS COUNCIL
ENGLAND   Peepal Tree gratefully acknowledges Arts Council support

CONTENTS

ACKNOWLEDGMENTS

Give thanks to the following publications in which the following stories were first published:

'Third Time' in *Avocado Magazine*.
'Who's Your Daddy?' in *Small Axe - A caribbean platform for criticism*.
'Beeline and Babylon' in *The Caribbean Writer*.
'Coward Men Keep Sound Bones' in *Asili: the Journal*.
'I Want to Disturb my Neighbor' in *Julie Mango Online Journal of Creative Expressions* & revised in *Iron Balloons: Fiction from Jamaica's Calabash Writer's Workshop*.
'Sister Faye and the Dreadlocked Vampire' in *OBSIDIAN: Literature in the African Diaspora*.

For Nadia

THIRD TIME

I'm a man who believes in signs, and that things come in threes, especially when it comes to people. It's like my father (may his soul rest in peace) taught me as he counted on his right hand, "Josh, all important things come in threes: mind, thought and action. The three things we will never understand: God, love, and death. The three things a man must do in this life: share his story, have a child, and plant a tree." I believed my father.

So last week when Alvaro Guzman walked into my office, I wasn't as surprised as he was when he saw me sitting in the chair he'd once sat in. Clean shaven, but still smelling of cigarettes (the only time he smoked was when he was nervous) with his hair slicked back, trying not to look like the man who had left the supermarket fifteen months ago, swearing he would never return to this *hijo'e puta* store, and that we could all go and fuck ourselves.

"Wazup, Josh?"

He pulled up a chair without asking for an invitation. That was Alvaro. He hadn't changed. He never asked for anything, and especially not from me. If he saw something he wanted, he took it. No questions asked. If he wanted the janitors to do something for him and they refused, he would hit them and they couldn't do anything because he would threaten to report them to the *La Migra*-INS. That was the first lesson he taught me when I came to work as a stockman in Howard's Supermarket where he worked as the assistant manager.

"I like you Haitians," he said.

"I'm Jamaican," I said – not because I wouldn't have been proud to be mistaken for Haitian, but you have to represent.

"Whatever. All I'm saying is you guys work hard, and I like that. But you guys lack one thing. *Cojones.* You know what that is?"

I pretended that I didn't. What Alvaro didn't know was that I'd studied Spanish and French at Jamaica College, the best high school in Jamaica. But due to "family problems", as my guidance counsellor said, I never graduated.

"Balls, man. Balls. You gotta have balls," and he grabbed his crotch to make his point, so I could understand. "You gotta be able to see what you want and grab it. You know, it's like a woman. You gotta grab her and say, 'Bitch, you're mine.' Women like that. That's how you gotta do it."

"I see."

I was a quick learner and Alvaro soon moved me from the floor and up the ladder until I was doing most of his work.

Soon, too, he was sharing his complaints about his fat wife, Liliana. All she did was lie around the house while he was out here breaking his back to bring home the bread, and when he wanted to have sex with her, she was always tired.

"That's all that *puta* does, man. Watch Jerry Springer and her *telenovelas* and when I come home, she's too tired to have sex. And when we do have sex, it's always *uno, dos, tres.* Which is all right with me. I get my load off, but damn! But that's all she does, man, stay home and watch that asshole."

Not that Alvaro wasn't getting enough sex. He had his little *sucia* down in Hialeah – which is why he promoted me so fast up the line, so he could take Fridays off to be with her and always have the alibi that he was working in the warehouse until midnight. It started off one Friday a month, but before long it was every Friday. I was keeping track of the inventory in the store while he was frying his *chorizo* in Hialeah.

That's how I got to meet Liliana or Lili, as she likes me to call her. Alvaro was going to make a delivery, as he called it, and he needed me to drop off the groceries at his house.

"You gotta help me out here, bro."

"But it's out of my way. I live way up in Carol City."

"Don't make me remind you of all the things I've gone out of my way to do for you."

The way he said it, I knew I couldn't refuse him or it would be my job. So, I said yes and, on my way home, I swung around to Alvaro's house in Miami Lakes.

The door was open, but I still knocked. Lili said to come in and I walked into a living room which was tastefully painted in whites, off-whites and creams, with bird of paradise flowers and sun-flowers on a table beside the bay window. I knew she'd designed it because Alvaro would sometimes show up for work (without even the excuse of coming straight from his *sucia's* house) wearing brown shoes, green-plaid pants, and a red-striped shirt. Like he was white!

Lili covered her legs with a nightgown that looked like it came from a Victoria's Secrets catalogue and continued doing her crossword puzzle and watching *Jeopardy*.

"What is the Battle of Hastings?" I said.

Lili was surprised. She looked up at me and uncrossed her legs. She had strawberry blond hair and a triangular face. She was a little overweight, but I wouldn't have thrown her out of my apartment if she left some crumbs in the bed.

"You're not Haitian."

"No."

"I can tell by your accent that you're Jamaican. Am I right?"

"Yes."

"Alvaro told me some Haitian guy was going to drop off the groceries. He said I should leave the door open so I wouldn't have to get up."

"That was kind of him."

She looked at me strangely, and took the box. I helped her unpack the groceries, answered a few more *Jeopardy* questions and helped her with the crossword puzzle.

"What are you doing working in Howard's Supermarket?"

"I'm saving to go into college."

"Which one?"

"Anyone. I'd like to go to UM, but it's a lot of money."

"Why don't you try Miami Dade?"

"Never. I've got too much pride."

She laughed and poured herself rum and Coke. She licked the tip of the index finger she'd used to stir the drink and took at sip while looking at me through the bottom of the glass. Lili was evidently the kind of woman who liked to feel that she was being admired.

She poured herself another, this time without the Coke, and offered me one.

"I don't drink and drive."

"You gotta take chances, kid. Or you'll wake up one day and find that your whole life is behind you."

I don't know where she got that "kid" from; I was twenty-one and she (I learned this later) was only six years older.

I left her when she filled up again. The ice cubes were melting faster than she could pour the rum.

Next day Alvaro was happy. His wife had gotten her groceries, and he had seen his *sucia*. Life couldn't have been better.

"My wife really likes you, man. Why didn't you tell me you weren't Haitian?"

"It must have slipped my mind," I said.

"Anyway, now that she trusts you, I can slip away every now and then. If I need you to deliver my groceries, you'll do it, right?"

"Yeah, sure, Alvaro. Anything you say."

"That's the spirit, man. You're a real team player. You're going to go a long way, man. I got plans for you."

For the next six months, I dropped off Alvaro's groceries every Friday and Lili and I did our bantering, our little innuendoes and jokes – until it happened.

In the middle of *Jeopardy*, as one of the contestants was saying, "Who is Abelard?" I kissed her and she kissed me back. After *Jeopardy*, we went downstairs to the laundry room (he was an asshole but I wasn't going to disrespect his bed) and we made love until the *Eleven O'clock Eyewitness News*, which gave me enough time to make my exit, because Alvaro liked to watch the opening monologue of *The Tonight Show* with Jay Leno.

That was the first and what I thought would the last time we'd make love, because Lili was so overcome with guilt that she said we must never do it again.

I kept on delivering the groceries though, so we wouldn't arouse Alvaro's suspicions. I started watching his every move, noting his every habit. I had to know him better than he knew himself. My life depended on it.

Still, all we did was kiss, and then she'd back off. I would go home horny and frustrated.

I did learn a lot, though, during the time when we didn't have sex. From the long conversations we had, I learned that she had been her class valedictorian and Alvaro had been a high-school baseball star who everyone thought would make it to the major leagues, but he never did. He lacked what the scouts called "the killer instinct". He played for Miami-Dade's baseball team and a few minor league teams, but never made it further.

In high school, though, Alvaro was the boy every girl wanted to date. He and Lili were crowned the king and queen of their graduating class. All their friends said that they made a great couple, so everything should have worked out.

On prom night they had sex in the limousine on the way back from a party on South Beach. Three months later she found out she was pregnant. Her mother was thrilled. Alvaro was the man for her. He was handsome, played baseball and his family had a lot of money. But as my father always said, "Any mother who tells her daughter to marry for money is only setting her up for the highest bidder."

But they did the right thing and got married with the blessing of both families and all of Hialeah. Two months later, Lili had a miscarriage. Now she was living with a man with whom she didn't want any children. After the miscarriage she became depressed. The doctor prescribed Prozac and recommended that she stay at home and take it easy for a while. She'd stayed home since then. But not because she wanted to stay, she just didn't know where she could go.

By this time they'd been married for nine years and since then her mother had died and so had Alvaro's father – so they'd inherited a nice house in Miami Lakes, but that was it. Lili told me she was like the rest of her friends – stuck in a marriage with a man she didn't love.

She asked me many times to run away with her, start a new life somewhere else. I told her I was tired of running.

It was an accusation I'd heard when I'd just turned twenty and was leaving Jamaica. One of the boys from our neighbourhood, Richard Silveira (whom I never liked because when we were younger his mother told him not to play with me because his great-grandfather once owned my great-grandfather), came up to me and said, "Why are you running away?". When I didn't answer he said, "Why do you want to live in a place where you'll always be treated as a second-class citizen?". "Second class like your mumma?" I said. "Second class only exists in your mind." He never talked to me again. I was glad.

But it wasn't just the running way that she wanted. Lili wanted a baby, but she wasn't going to have a baby with a man who, she said, was "Born missing the corn in the *arepas*", and always used brute force to get what he wanted.

I wanted to have a child, but I was afraid. Lili was the kind of woman who would inflict the same troubles she'd inherited from her mother on her own children. Parents always mess up their kids. But you shouldn't mess up kids with their grandparents' problems – they should be your own. Lili had messed up her life by following her mother's advice. She'd liked a boy named Daniel, but according to her mother Daniel wasn't going anywhere. Alvaro was different. He was "the chosen one".

Lili's mother could only see money. When Lili told her that Alvaro had slapped her when she didn't have his dinner ready, her mother invited him over and fed him herself.

"Why don't you marry my mother? You spend so much time with her."

"Your mom knows how to treat a man. When I go over there, she always has a meal ready for me, even if it's only rice with an egg on top. It's not like here where I gotta make the shit if I want to eat!"

Now Lili wanted a change. The difference between her and me is that she knows what she wants, but only after she's lost it. I know what I want. I just don't know if I'll get it.

We continued tearing at each other for six months without having sex. Then the owner of the supermarket, Howard Foster, found out that Alvaro was never there and that I was doing all his work. Howard called Alvaro into his office, but before he could say anything, Alvaro told him to stick the job up his white ass. He knew what was going to happen. He told me he was leaving Florida forever.

Everyone in the store, especially the cleaning ladies who he was always threatening to fire if they didn't have sex with him, was happy. Everyone except me.

It was then that Lili and I had sex for the second time, this time in their bedroom because I was sure that Alvaro wasn't coming back that night, and I thought I'd never see her again. She cried and said she was going to miss me (I felt like crying too, but I didn't let on). I asked her if she knew where they were going to live. She said she didn't know, but that she was going with Alvaro. She was a brave woman.

It wasn't until six months later (after the owner of the supermarket, facing bankruptcy, sold the store to a Haitian man, Frantz La Fontaine) that I heard from Lili again. I told her about all the things that had happened, that I'd been promoted to manager of the stores and that I was going part-time to school at Miami Dade. She said she was proud of me, and that she always knew I would go places.

I don't know about that. I just work hard and apply what my mother said (I will not speak ill of the dead even though she ran off with my father's best friend): "If you can't make the world a better place, at least clean up after yourself!"

Lili told me they were now living in New Orleans and that things were bearable since Alvaro had found a new girlfriend in the French Quarter.

And then, Katrina…

"So are you going to hire me or are you going to make me beg? Cause I ain't gonna beg even though Liliana said that I should."

I hired Alvaro on the spot. It was a sign. The third time was near.

One day I'll plant a tree and have a child. But for now, I'm waiting. Sooner or later, Alvaro will go back to his old habits and ask for some time off to see his old *sucia* in Hialeah or find a new one, and I will grant him the time just because of the "good old days". And while he's stacking the Purina Cat Chow in the warehouse, I will be having sex with his wife on the dining room floor or in his bed again. For as my father always said, "The third time's the charm."

FIRST LOVE

Mark watched Patrick as he entered the showers and wondered how it would feel to have Patrick's arm around his waist and the ripple of his thighs against his buttocks.

For two weeks that had been all he could think about as they took the long walk from Manning Cup football practice (on the bottom field of JC) and passed the newly-built chemistry and physics lab while the groundsmen mowed the grass on "Holy Ground".

As the shadow of Long Mountain fell across the trunks of the Australian pines gathering the amber light dying on the corrugated roofs of Standpipe, they trampled over the grass soaked by an afternoon squall that had drenched the field, but had not stopped their game.

"They were sufferin'; rude boys gave them Bufferin!"

Their raucous hoots seemed to mock the Latin inscription – *Fervet Opus In Campis* – over Scott Hall and the austere names of the houses – Cowper, Musgrave, Hardy and Murray – JC's homage to the English boarding-school tradition.

Mark had been in top form that afternoon, making impossible saves seem ordinary, orchestrating attacks from the goal line by lobbing the ball to Patrick, his midfielder, or organizing the defence behind Charles, his sweeper. Although they played for different houses during the school year, they came together for their practice match as if they hadn't missed a beat.

"Blood claat game," said Charles. He banged his cleats against the bench with the same ferocity that he showed when he was sulking over a lost game. Yet they had won; Mark was confused.

"Are you going to mash up everything?"

"No, no, something on my mind. You made some great saves today, man!"

The rest of the team joined in. If they had not respected Mark's ability before, his performance that afternoon made them realize why the boys in the lower school had nicknamed him the "football *ginigog*". He was almost certain of a place on Jamaica's national football team – something also anticipated by Mark's own family.

Mark lived and breathed football. From primary school he'd shown signs of surpassing his older brother and cousin, both of whom had played for Jamaica during the early sixties. Much more than his brother and cousin (both as tall as he was – six feet two) he knew how to use his size to intimidate opponents.

When Mark let out his blood-curdling scream, "My ball!" and left his goal line, there weren't many strikers who challenged him. He had done this twice that afternoon and both times the striker had just curled up "like a pussy" (according to Charles) and allowed Mark to get the ball.

Now, though, there were other things on Mark's mind. He kept going over and over how Patrick's hands had met his in the dark when they had gone with Patrick's cousins, Jennifer and Althea, to see *Lethal Weapon 2*.

Patrick had leaned over and whispered, "Where there's a will, there's a weapon", and touched his hand. It had happened so fast that Mark wasn't sure if it was the attraction or the danger that excited him.

And it was dangerous. It didn't matter that he was the best goalie in Kingston. Even though he was the captain of the football team, he still went to JC, and the school, since its founding in 1789, had always had a reputation for harbouring gay teachers and students. Even now, after the government of Michael Manley (himself a JC alumnus) dismantled the entrance rules that had only allowed the sons of the white landed class and the sons of the brown middle class to enter JC's hallowed halls (which led to Patrick's father saying that Manley had betrayed his race and class), every JC boy was still suspect.

Just the week before, while Mark and his teammates were waiting in the bleachers of the National Stadium for a game against Calabar, the KC boys (whom JC had recently beaten) – up in the highest section of the bleachers – were throwing peanuts at them and singing:

> Don't let batty boys invite you to dinner
> Or you will become a sinner
> Don't let batty boy give you bread and jelly
> It will give you pain in you belly
> Batty boy jelly Oh. Don't want no batty boy jelly Oh
> Batty boy jelly will give pain in you belly Oh!

Despite Charles's advice not to respond to the taunts, Mark had jumped out of his seat and screamed. "We beat you six-love! How does it feel to be beaten by batty boys?"

He thought that would have quieted them. It did for a while, until one the KC boys shouted, "So, you're admitting that you're batty boys!"

The stands exploded in laughter and the KC boys began hurling paper cups and peanut shells at them – anything they could get their hands on. Mark and his teammates had to run for cover and wait in the changing rooms for the game to begin.

When the JC team came out to play, Patrick was so angry that he fought for every ball remotely near him – something he never did in any other game – and scored three goals against Calabar.

"Not bad for a group of batty boys," Coach Thompson joked.

But it was no joking matter. In third form, they had all heard the story of how some of the prefects had caught and beaten "a Chinee batty boy". The boy had been injured so badly he had to be rushed to the emergency room. He never came back to the school.

Now as they passed the prefects' hall, under the shade of a Bombay mango tree in full bloom, a shudder went through Mark's body, but as they entered the changing rooms he could think only of Patrick's muscular thighs.

As he bent over and began loosening the laces of his boots and cleaning the mud from his cleats, the smell of sweat and the mildew that had already spread through the newly-built locker and stalls assailed him.

Glancing over at the shower stalls, he noticed that Patrick had left the latch open. He was always the first in and the last out. Charles had told him that unlike the rest of them, Patrick was circumcised and didn't want to be seen naked to add to the list of the things – like his blond hair and grey eyes – that already made him different from the other boys.

How did Charles know this?

As he pulled the top laces on his boots, he studied the initials that Vivian "Dog head" Samuels had carved into the wood and embellished with the shape of a woman's vulva. He traced his finger along the edges of the carving, admiring the handiwork, and wondered if Vivian had used a chisel stolen from the art room.

Whap!

The wet towel stung against his buttocks. It had to be Charles.

"Shit, man, how many times I have to tell you don't do that. It hurts."

"Had to get you out of your slumber, man. Were you thinking about the girl 'Dog head' used as a model, or about Patrick?"

"What do you mean?"

"You looked over at the stalls like you wanted to kill him. You must have heard what he's been saying about you."

"What's that?"

"All kind of fuckry. But you know me, I won't let anybody talk badly about you. Me and you go way back."

They did. He and Charles had been friends since primary school, but when they entered JC, Charles had been placed in Hardy House and he in Murray. When they became the football captains of their respective houses, their rivalry had created something of a rift. Now in the lower sixth, they'd been further separated into arts and sciences.

Mark had a natural gift for mathematics and breezed through his chemistry and physics classes. Charles, on the other hand, was taking literature, history, and geography.

"Man, I don't see you any more. The only time we see each other is at training and then you run off with your little friend, Patrick."

Charles ran his fingers through his hair and the curled wisps around his ears. Mark wondered if he was going to grow dreadlocks as he said he would once he got to sixth form.

"C'mon man. "A" levels are coming up. You and Patrick are going to study *Hamlet* together."

"I just don't want to be studying with that white boy. That boy thinks he can say and do anything just because his father is the president of the Old Boys Association."

"C'mon Charles, what's with the white boy business? He didn't go to primary school with us, but we've all known each other since first form."

"You wouldn't know, Mark. You're brown and they don't say the same things around you."

"Like what?"

"Like when I showed up late for biology class, Patrick's batty boy uncle, Mr. Silveira, said, 'Since when have they let the groundsman's son into JC?' Fuckry, like that."

"Charles, that was four years ago. I thought you'd forgotten that."

"You don't forget about these things. They stay with you."

Charles held onto grudges like that. Mark knew he'd always find a way to get even with anyone who slighted him. If he didn't like someone, or if he felt that they'd got something he should have gotten, he'd find out something bad about them – or make it up – and spread rumours. Mark was just glad that Charles didn't hold it against him that he'd been named as captain of the Manning Cup team and was now headed for the All Stars team.

"Patrick's not like that."

"Don't tell me you're taking up for him. Not after what he's been saying"

Charles eyes tightened and now he looked almost like his mother, Miss Chin Loy, whom his father never married because "it didn't look right". Charles had never told anyone about his family, except Mark.

"What's he been saying about me?"

Mark laughed and shook his head.

"You don't want to know. He' a little batty boy."

"If they're saying he's a batty boy, what are they saying about me?"

"Nobody's saying you're a batty boy. We all know you're a baller – although you do like the white girls."

"How?"

"I know about you and his cousins. But we've been watching him and how he's been looking at you."

So Patrick had been watching him.

"The way I just saw you looking at him, I know you feel like murdering him yourself."

Murder was not the word.

"So tell me, what did he say?"

"That you let him score on you last week."

It was true. In the last minutes of the inter-house championship, Patrick had got the ball away from one of Mark's defenders. Their eyes had met. Mark purposely dove to his right when he knew that Patrick was going to kick the ball to the left.

"What!"

"Yeah, man. Yeah."

He had allowed Patrick to score as sign of his trust, but the way Patrick's teammates behaved, it was as if they had won the championship.

"He said that you'd given up the goal for him – and you're the best goalie this school has seen in a long time."

"That little…"

"Batty boy."

Mark could count on the fingers of one hand all the players who'd scored on him for the six years he had been at JC and consoled himself that all of them had gone on to play for the national team. Patrick was good, but not that good.

"Everybody but *you* knows he's a batty boy. We can't prove it, but *we* know it. We're going trap him."

"Fuck off, Charles. I'm not getting involved in any batty boy business."

"You don't have to do anything, man. His own batty boy self will give him away. We're just going leave the room."

"No, I don't want to be involved."

"It's already set, Mark. It's happening today. I'm telling you this because I'm your friend. That white batty boy is going to get a beating tonight."

"No."

"It's too late. We all know that you're a baller. He's the one who's suspect," Charles said as he left the room.

Patrick was still in the showers.

The leaves of the Bombay mango tree scraped across the roof of the changing room, sending dried pollen through the window.

Mark coughed.

The showers stopped.

"Mark?"

Mark wanted to tell Patrick to stop, not to come out of the showers, but he could only cough.

"Mark, are you all right?"

Patrick came out of the showers with his towel wrapped around his waist. Mark looked at him and turned his back.

"Is anyone else here?"

Mark was trembling now. He wanted to say something, but didn't or couldn't. He wanted to scream, but didn't.

"Are you okay?"

Patrick was behind him. Mark could hear his own heartbeat. It was louder than the sound of the lawnmower that had edged closer to the changing rooms.

Patrick touched him on the shoulder and he shuddered. Yes, it was real despite the danger. He couldn't turn around. Patrick massaged his shoulders and pulled at the towel, but Mark held the edge.

"No!"

Mark's cry echoed through the changing rooms and Charles and the rest of his teammates came running in.

"No!"

Patrick tried to escape by climbing out the window, but Charles and his teammates grabbed him by the arms, dragged him to the ground and began beating him with their fists and kicking him with their boots. Charles grabbed Patrick's head and began beating it against the concrete floor.

"Mark you don't want a piece of this?"

Patrick looked up at Mark and their eyes met as they had at the moment when Patrick had the chance to score and Mark had let him. Patrick looked at him for some kind of acknowledgement, as if he could bear this beating if Mark would only give him some sign.

Mark would not. Patrick had brought this on himself and Mark could not give that sign, not now, not ever.

Mark kicked Patrick in the groin.

Patrick doubled over and the rest of the boys joined in a frenzy of blows over Patrick's body. They beat him until he was unconscious. He lay on the floor, naked and bloody.

One of the boys asked, "Should we cover him or something?"

Charles said, "No, leave him for the groundsmen to find. He got what he deserved. Nasty batty boy."

"Yeah," said Mark. "Nasty batty boy."

"He's my soul mate," said Angie. "And I do deserve some happiness in my life…"

She squeezed Roy's hand, which hung limply from the railing of the hospital bed.

I didn't know what to say. Angie, who'd been through two failed marriages ending in a suicide and a divorce, still managed to keep the air of dignity that the nuns at school had said ladies should always have, but which some people in church equated as cold and unfeeling. Some went a bit further and called her a "calculating bitch". Unlike those people, I don't think she planned anything.

Two years ago, her pastor had asked her to visit a new member, a widower, who'd recently suffered a mild heart attack. But when she got to the hospital, Roy was already sitting up in bed with his teenage son, Clive, at his side.

"I made it without using this."

He dangled his No-CPR bracelet.

Angie introduced herself and, after a few minutes of small talk, she realized they had many things in common. They'd both been born in Montego Bay during the fifties, came to Miami in their twenties, and they both loved old movies – especially *Casablanca*.

"I'll leave you two alone," said Clive when he realized they had started a conversation that excluded him.

They were also fascinated by their differences – many of which they discovered on a long date at the *Fontainebleau* that started at eight at night and lasted until six in the morning. He'd grown up poor and black; she brown and rich. He'd left Jamaica as a single man to seek opportunities while she'd left with her husband to preserve their wealth. Whilst the Lozano riots were rocking Miami, Roy was still living with Clive's mother in the black neighbourhood of Liberty City, while Angie, recently divorced, was living in Westchester and passing for Hispanic. When Hurricane Andrew devastated South Florida, Angie lost her second husband and the new restaurant they'd just opened. By then, Roy was a successful real estate agent living in Broward and waiting for the "white flight," that would make him a multimillionaire.

In a very brief time, they realized they had a lifetime of catching up to do and seeing the world through each other's eyes.

During their six months of courtship, Angie enjoyed the things that life had taken away from her. After the seventh month, Angie suggested that they should get married. She hated being scandalized by folk at the church, and didn't want "to live in sin".

At first, Roy wanted to wait until Clive turned twenty-one – the age when *his* father had told him he was on his own. Eventually, they agreed on a compromise. Angie would sign a prenuptial. If Roy died before Clive turned twenty-one, Clive would inherit Roy's wealth.

They went on their honeymoon to Jamaica, and visited Angie's old "stomping grounds", places Roy had never known existed.

During the second week away, Roy stopped taking his heart medicine without telling Angie, and one night he sent her up to bed so he could stay up with some old buddies he wanted to impress. He had one Appleton too many.

When Angie got the call from the lobby, Roy was already slipping into a coma, and she did what any survivor would have done. She slipped the No-CPR bracelet off his wrist, called a doctor who revived him, flew him back to Kingston, and put him under the care of her doctor.

Clive had fought in the courts for his father's return to Miami; his twenty-first birthday was near.

"You understand, don't you?"

Roy's ventilator wheezed with each rise and fall.

WHO'S YOUR DADDY?

Every morning after *The Howard Stern Show*, I'd have to stand on the corner of Miami Gardens and 20th to wait for the school bus to take me on a ride for an hour and a half to a school that's really only twenty minutes away. By car, even in the worst traffic, it takes thirty minutes, tops. I timed it when Arnold, my stepfather, used to drive my ex-girlfriend, Susan and me to school. That was when he used to live with us, before he left me, my mom, our house and everything behind.

So I had to take the bus and deal with the driver, Ms. Fletcher, a big, fat, white woman (she didn't even know I was absent for two weeks), and make my way to the back of the bus to face even more humiliation.

For the two weeks I was absent, she'd probably stopped, opened the door for the designated seven seconds that her union says it takes for a kid to get on the bus and take a seat. It never changed. When she screams at a kid (in violation of school-board rules), it's always, "Get your ass down, you piece of shit!" But I guess she has to talk that way to us, which is how everyone speaks to us, for anything else would be taken as a sign of weakness. And I, too, hate weakness.

It's like when my mom finally persuaded me to go and see the ninth grade guidance counsellor because of my truancy, and the counsellor asked me, "Michael, why are you so angry? Your life isn't that bad!"

"How would you know?"

"Because other children in this school have gone through worse than what you've been through and they haven't spent the past month threatening other kids."

When she said that, I clammed up.

"Did you mean what you said about mailing anthrax to your classmates? I don't know if you know this, but it's a federal offence to joke about something like that out loud, much less threaten someone. But I know you're a good boy. You really didn't mean it, did you?"

I didn't answer her. She didn't deserve an answer. She's just collecting her paycheck every two weeks and then goes home to her fat, loser husband; they have fat, loser sex, and pretty soon they'll have fat, loser kids like those that surround me in this fat, loser school. Besides, she seems to think that I don't know that I'm a genius.

But that morning, as I made my way through the gauntlet of white kids to the back of the bus, they started teasing me again, "He showed you who was the man. He showed you, you Bill Gates wannabe." I didn't want a fight that morning so all I could do was hold my book bag close to my body and slump into my seat for what seemed an eternity.

Besides, they're all imbeciles.

When we finally got off the bus and I stepped out into the parking lot, the old fear came over me again. I hesitated. The thought of spending a day in that dreadful school (it had no windows and no ventilation) sickened me. The school, which is supposed to be one of the best in the county (an "A" school on the governor's FCAT list), is the official hurricane evacuation centre for Aventura. Back in the sixties, it was a bomb shelter in case of a nuclear attack (yeah, right). As if concrete could stop the effects of radiation. What were they thinking?

I walked through the hallways (more teasing and jibes) and went straight to the homeroom (even more teasing and jibes) and had to sit through three hours of that shit. Three hours. Three hours of shit because now they had something they could pin on me. Before, I'd had nothing they could tease me about (except being a geek – my fascination with computers) but now I was vulnerable. Susan had given them something they could use against me. Something real and personal. Something they could use to defeat me. I had no choice.

I should never have fallen in love with her. But it was inevitable. The first time I really saw her was when we were in PE. She had brown hair and pale, almost translucent skin – I could see the capillaries in her forearm. And her hands. Her fingers were long and slender and I loved to see them dance across the keys when she practised at home, even when she was playing "Für Elise" or something corny like that. Susan was was totally real. That was what I liked about her. She wasn't like those other JAPS who wore a lot of make-up, jewellery and were totally fake. But they never wanted to see us together because Susan was white and Jewish and I was black and Jamaican.

But Susan liked me because I'm smarter than all the other kids in the class. I see things and call things for what they are without any bullshit. Nothing scares me – not power, not money. "I'm a Buffalo Soldier, dreadlocked Rasta." I could be Marcus Garvey or John Malvo. Well, not really, my mom won't let me have dreadlocks because she says we're not low-class Jamaican ragamuffins.

"I've left all of that behind me, Michael. I didn't leave Jamaica for you to come here and become a Rasta. I don't care what everyone else has to say about Bob Marley. I never liked his music. And there's nothing romantic about poverty. You just remember that. I know poverty. You haven't. I've given you everything that you need and it just burns me up that you're not talking advantage of all the sacrifices I've made for you. Why you can't help me, boy? Is not like we're back home where I could have somebody to help me with you. Is just me and you alone."

At that point I tuned her out because I didn't want to hear, *Oh, all the things that I've done for you*, ever again. She was always trying to make me better than I was. So what?

Susan loved me for me. She wasn't into the whole money thing. Sure, she had money, but her parents were hippies. She wore long dresses and Birkenstocks and on the day I first saw her, the wind was blowing her dress over her head. I was thinking, "Blow west wind, blow."

I waited for three hours until Bobby finally showed up to our history class. Bobby (Roberto is his real name) is the commissioner's son. He wasn't supposed to be in our school because it's overcrowded, but because he's the big guy's son, he was here with us – a real paino in the ass-so.

He thought he was special because he could afford all the latest clothes and was always bragging about where his family went every weekend. His father was grooming him to become the first Cuban-American president. He was on the debating team and played shortstop on the baseball team. All the girls thought he was cute because his father was so powerful and all the mothers wanted their daughters to be with him to become the First Lady or something. Tough luck.

And he would have been president. He walked around bullying all the kids, pushing them, and saying nasty things to them. He thought he was smart, but I knew I was smarter. The rest of them were just playing at being smart. Like Bob Marley said, "A whole lot of people are living off false pretences." Well, I wasn't one of them. I never fronted in my life. Never will.

That's why my other classmates didn't stand up to Bobby when he said things like, "Your family's so poor, you step on a cockroach and someone says, 'Who killed the family pet?'" Or "Your family's so poor, someone steps on a cigarette and they say, 'Who turned off the heat?'" They didn't do anything, or say anything because he has the principal, the teachers, the security, this whole fucking school behind him. And when he'd finished demolishing them, he'd say, "Who's *your* Daddy?" like he was Eminen or somebody like that. He thought he was so powerful. He thought he was so smart. He had everything. But I wasn't scared of him. I didn't give a shit about all that.

I first came into the class from JFK Middle (Jail for Kids we called it) eight weeks ago. I was happier there. I was in regular classes and coasting through and I didn't have to put up with all this bullshit of being the only black kid in the class.

I never wanted to be with these white kids who eat in a separate cafeteria, use different bathrooms, have everything different. The schools use the honours program to have white kids and black kids in the same school and then they say we're *integrated*. They should call it for what it is – segregation. I don't mind it; they just shouldn't be hypocrites.

My mom finally made me agree to be tested by the guidance counsellor who said the reason for my aggression was because I was bored. And they paid her how much to figure that out? I promised my mother I would do my best this time (I'd blown off all the others) and took the test. Surprise, surprise, I scored off the charts. I had the highest percentile scores in the class, and I didn't have a private tutor and Kaplan Testing behind me. See, money can't buy you everything. Well, it can't buy you brains.

I sized him up from the first day of class and I waited and waited until he finally picked on me (didn't take him long). Bobby came around and tried to insult me. He never figured I'd defend myself. So when he started with his usual lame insults, I countered them easily. Then I started in on him. I ripped him apart verbally. Any slight physical deformity of his eyes, ears, or nose I exaggerated. I told him that guys with small noses and small ears had small dicks. I gouged out his eyes. When I was finished with his physical appearance, I stripped away every mental façade that he'd erected. I made fun of the lingering accent he still had (from speaking only Spanish at home) and totally demolished him. I destroyed, decapitated, and decimated him. He never had a chance. He was no match for me. And when he tried to hit me, I put a move on him that Arnold had taught me, and floored him.

Mr. Jordan, our history teacher, didn't report the incident. He liked me. He asked me who had taught me the move, and I told him it was my step dad. I liked Mr. Jordan. He reminded me a lot of Arnold. Both of them had served in Vietnam and both of them told me real stories about the war. Things that really happened. I was always asking them questions and Mr. Jordan, whenever he didn't feel like teaching, would put down the textbook and tell us stories about Vietnam and we'd spend the rest of the period talking about the war. Mr. Jordan was the one who told me about his capture by the Vietnamese. He didn't tell them anything. Even when he was in prison and they tortured him for three years, they didn't get a word out of him. They didn't deserve the truth, he said.

Arnold used to tell me stories about the war too. He was a sniper. He'd told me how it looked when he popped a guy's head open from over a hundred meters away. Brains and blood all over the place. He was so cool about it. He said it straight up, without excitement, like he was pouring a cup of coffee or something like that. He didn't flinch.

He always said, as he looked at me with his slate coloured eyes that had seen so much killing, "The government paid me to smoke weed and kill gooks. Best gig I ever had."

I thought Arnold was a really cool guy because he took the time to talk with me. I thought he was way cooler than my dad, a car salesman who couldn't keep his dick in his pants, and slept with every woman who worked with him. When I asked him why he did it, he said, "A dick doesn't have a conscience, son." I never saw him again.

Arnold made me believe he was here to stay, but when I found out he was cheating on my mom, I had to let her know the truth.

He deserved it. He shouldn't have called me "The Snoop". I may be a snoop, but he shouldn't have called me that. I know everything that goes on in this neighbourhood. I know Mr. Samuels comes out some mornings at three or four in the morning (usually when I'm surfing the web) to have a smoke even though he's had three heart attacks and should have quit two years ago. I know Mrs. Ortega, who cut her hair a month ago, skips over the fence every Friday to see Mr. Reid when she's supposed to be on her lunch break. What I can't understand is why Mrs. Ortega (such a good-looking woman) would want to be with a fat, old loser like Mr. Reid. I guess I'm too young or something, but I'll never understand the choices women make about the guys they sleep with.

That's why I could never understand when Susan told me that Bobby had been her ex. Not that I was expecting her to be waiting around for me to come along. But Bobby! He never showered after baseball games and nobody had the nerve to tell him he smelled because they were afraid of him. The next time I saw him I planned to tell him. I'm not afraid to tell the truth.

That's how my mom and I are different. When I found out that Arnold was having an affair with my mom's best friend, Fat Monica, and paid for the trysts on a credit card he kept hidden from my mom, I exposed him.

I found out about the affair one morning when I hacked into his online account and saw all the hotel bills for a Howard Johnson near the house. I knew he wasn't with my mom. He'd been screwing Fat Monica (another one I'll never figure out) for the past year, every Thursday, when he was supposed to be in the gym trying to control his cholesterol.

I sent my mom an e-mail for her to meet him the following Thursday in the lobby of the hotel. The three of them showed up and that was the end of that. Stupid people deserve all that they have coming to them.

When Arnold tried to get back with my mom, I e-mailed his credit card accounts to her, like it was mistake from the credit card company, but that started another fight. He left without his bicycle, his bowling ball, and, of course, his gun.

I found his gun in the loft. I needed a new place to escape from their fights – my knuckles were raw from banging them into the wall. I was tired of him calling my mom "a cold bitch". He said he wouldn't have started with Monica if my mom hadn't been so uptight about everything. I slipped into the crawlspace without anyone noticing, trying to get the thought out of my mind that my mom could actually be at fault for the breakup when I found his .38 beside a pile of *Playboys* and *Hustlers*. All the time he was supposed to be fixing the air conditioner and putting down the insulation, he was up there whacking off.

My mom, when she finally called the cops and got a restraining order against him, packed his bags and dropped them off at the hotel where he used to see Monica. I guess he figured no one would ever find the gun, but I did! (My mom told him before they got married she didn't want the gun in the house and he'd told her he'd pawned it.) Anyway, he never came back for anything.

But that's when things started to go downhill. My mom, a legal secretary, had to work overtime to pay the bills and I began to see less and less of her. When I did see her, she was sleeping. Just recently she'd taken on a filing job for an accountant in Fort Lauderdale. One night she told me, before she dozed off, that this accountant guy wants to meet me. But she's lying. I know she's still seeing Arnold.

We were about to lose the house because Arnold refused to pay alimony. He said he'd prefer not to work than to pay alimony. And he didn't work. My mom slipped behind the mortgage payments (even with a VA loan) and everything was slipping away. We were losing everything and it was all my fault. Then he started sending her e-mail, which I intercepted, and I found out that they were seeing each other behind my back. She was whoring it up – though she'd probably say it was for my sake. I'm not taking the blame for that!

But I shouldn't have looked in her e-mail. Or I should have looked away, but I couldn't look away.

That's what got me in trouble with Bobby. Two weeks after I demolished him, Bobby sent me an e-mail with an attachment. I didn't want to open it, but the subject line was: I ate your girlfriend and she loved it!

I finally opened the attachment. It was a video clip. I saw what I had feared. I saw Bobby with his head of curls between Susan's legs and he was chomping down on her, and then looking up at the camera, winking and going back to work, then saying, "Did you really think you could have her, nigger? I popped this cherry! She's mine forever. You will never have her because I was her first. Losers finish last or get sloppy seconds."

He'd done it. Even though I was smarter than he was, getting better grades than he was without even trying, he'd called me a nigger. And not like, "Yo, my nigger, what's up" – as if he could. When he said it, he meant it to kill.

In the video, Susan looked groggy and later she told me he'd put something in her drink.

"But what were you doing at his house in the first place?"

"Me and Jenny were invited specially to come over to his house after a baseball game. You never go to the games and we'd won, so I decided to go with her for the celebration. But when we got there, it was only Bobby and a couple of his friends. They offered us some drinks, and then I can't remember anything."

"Did you tell your mom what happened?"

"No. I told her I was going to see Bobby because I didn't want her to suspect that anything was happening between us. I wanted her to think that Bobby and I had gotten back together."

"And you never figured anything like could happen with you and Bobby in the house?"

"I don't know."

"Or you didn't want to. I hate you and you deserve all that's coming to you."

But I was lying, of course. I couldn't hate her. After we'd made love for the first time and I was lying naked in bed with my right nipple against her shoulder, I realized I could never love anyone like I loved her. Even if she was Bobby's ex.

I'd tried to hate her because now we had to keep our love a secret. We'd tried to be honest and she'd told her dad about us. I always thought he was cool. Whenever, I went over to his house, he treated me with respect and was always saying, "Thanks for helping Susan with her homework. Susan says you're the smartest boy in the class."

But when she told her parents that we wanted to go steady, her father went ballistic. He asked her if she'd kissed me or anything else. He told her I was never to come back over to the house and if we continued seeing each other they were going to send her to private school.

"He used the N-word, Michael. The N-word. I never knew my father was such a racist bigot. Oh, I hate him. Hate him. I hate him!"

She told her parents that we'd stopped seeing each other. She, too, had started to lie.

On my first day back in Mr. Jordan's class, I put my book bag on the floor like I'd been planning for the past two weeks. Susan, then Bobby came into the room. Susan was kind of happy to see me, but when Bobby saw me, he sneered, "Come back for more punishment?"

Of course, he didn't call me a nigger to my face in class – he wouldn't have been cool any more. He just looked at me, trying to make me feel small when he didn't know it was just making me angrier. The hypocrite!

I don't take the blame for anything that happened after that. I was going to make him eat that sneer. I pulled Arnold's .38 out of my book bag and said to Bobby, "You'll never use your mouth again," and shot him in the face. Then I shot him in the balls. Then I shot him in the stomach and emptied the chamber into his chest. I didn't flinch.

"And besides, you smell too."

I was starting to reload. Everyone was under their desks. I grabbed Susan.

She asked, "Michael, what are you doing?"

I pulled her down on the floor, and took out the two bullets that I'd saved for her and for me.

"Taste this. Taste this. This is the bullet that's going to kill you. But before I kill you, I want you to take it into your mouth the way he took you into his and they way you took him…"

"But I never!"

"Whatever you did or you didn't, it doesn't really matter now does it?"

I pushed the bullet up to her face and she started to cry. She was weak. I loved her, but she was weak. Now she would pay the price for being weak.

"Suck on it. Suck on it!"

But she wouldn't.

Then as I was about to press it into her mouth, she looked at me and touched my hand.

"I never meant to hurt you, Michael."

That was when I lost it. I began banging my head against the wall and when I turned to face her, Mr. Jordan tackled me.

I didn't see him.

He brought me down and I tried the same move on him that I'd done with Bobby, but he countered it. He pinned me to the ground and kept me there until the cops came to take me to juvie.

He asked, "Why'd you do it, son?" Like he was my father or something. "Why'd you do it?"

I didn't answer him. He'd never understand. Now *he* doesn't deserve an answer. All I was thinking about as the cops put the handcuffs on my wrists was the spot where Susan had touched me.

SUNDAY MORNING, COMING DOWN

Let me tell you, rude boy, about the Sunday morning I was going to church with me son. I was worried about the boy. Him was doing all the things that boys do everywhere. But we was in Miami and I wasn't too sure that things mean the same like they do back in Jamaica. Here in Miami, up could mean down, and down could mean up. If I was confused, I could imagine how things was for him. So, I make the sacrifice every Sunday to go to church (even though back home I only went on Easter Sunday and Christmas) for although a whole heap of things change, I had to make sure the boy would grow up right.

We was sitting in traffic, air conditioning going full blast – white people in front of me, white people in the back, white people to me left, and white people to me right. I didn't know if I should run or stand up and fight.

Then, all of a sudden in the bright, bright Miami sun, perched on the back of a motorbike and hugging a jacket and helmet, the sweetest batty God ever put on a woman just haul up beside me. I wanted to roll down the window, but I didn't know if my son was looking, and I have to set an example, so all I could do was prips it through the window.

Rude boy, what a glorious batty the gyal did have. So round, so nice, so sweet, it would put marble to shame. It was the kind of batty that my wife don't like, for she say batty like that will lead me to places I shouldn't go any more. Well, at least, not since I married.

The gyal did have the kind of batty that take me back to Half-Way-Tree on a Friday afternoon waiting for a Jolly Joseph, patty pan, or minibus to rumble up from Hagley Park Road to the tune of Scotty's "Draw you Brakes" and the dawtas would be dancing the "S-90 Skank", "Cripple Skank" or the "Duck Walk" that make the *glammity* fat quiver like Port Royal earthquake all over again.

Lawd, what a magnificent batty! Make you want to smoke a spliff even though you never smoke – not even a cigarette – one day in your life! It was the kind of batty that would make you swear off food in the middle of a all-you-can-eat restaurant – it would make a rumhead bawl like you dash way him last bottle of Appleton and now him have to drink Limacol.

It was a boldface and bumptious batty. The kind that would make a sailor seasick – the way it rock and bounce from side to side, yet stand firm in one place. Here, there and everywhere, yet always at the centre. It was like God. It was the kind of batty that if you took it to church, it would make the sisters turn them face and gossip and would make the brothers wake up in the back of the church.

And then, slowly, quietly, I had a feeling like a warm blanket covering my neck. As I look over me shoulder, there was my boy looking at the gyal with the biggest grin on him face, like a mongoose in a chicken coop. And I feel good, for I realize right there that everything was irie. For on that Sunday morning, him and me was going have to fork out a whole heap of extra money for the offering plate to pay for the sin that was on we mind.

But still, all I can say is Hallelu, Hallelu, Hallelujah. Praise Jah.

BEELINE AGAINST BABYLON

Night was crowding the tamarind trees round the *Blue Heaven Hotel*, just before the peenie wallies started the light show above the blossoms of the lignum vitae. Beeline, my partner, that old dread, who had been a waiter, a landlord, a small investor, a drinker, a good fellow, a storyteller, somebody's baby father, somebody's yard boy, something in a bakery, a tax-gatherer, a bankrupt, a ship captain's assistant, a cook, a lifeguard, a taxi man, and now head security guard at the hotel – all to keep body, mind, soul and him family together – was sitting across the table from me on a seat that him make from a Seven-Up crate and playing a hand of dominoes. We was tied with Malcolm and Desmond at five all – which was almost like losing in Beeline book – with a hundred dollars in the pot and one game to go, when, all of a sudden, Babylon with gun, rifle and soldier broke down the door of Beeline shack down by the river and where him son Malcolm was sleeping.

The domino game look like it was going end though no one did know what Beeline was going do when we see them handcuff Malcolm and lead him through the gate. All Beeline could do at the time was sit down and watch, for him was afraid them might shoot or arrest him too. And we couldn't say a thing. We all did know that from the time him was a little boy, Malcolm used to get inna nuff trouble with the people in the village. Not bad trouble, just nuff trouble. I swear him give that old dread more grey hair than him could count – though now most of them was falling out. But this time the trouble was different. This time it involved the law and everybody know that despite everything else, Beeline respected the law. Him was a good man.

One time him and me go to the grocery store and them did have peanut for sale. Two for a dollar. Beeline start eat one in the store, and then him see one of him old time friend in the street. Him put the one unopened pack of peanuts in my basket, give me twenty dollar, and go talk with him friend. When I come outside with everything paid for, him realize that him never pay for he peanut him did start, so him go back to the store and return the peanut him pay for to replace the one him eat.

"What you do that for? It was only fifty cents."

"Fifty cents or five million. A thief is a thief and wrong is wrong," him say. Beeline would never thief or rob anyone, and everyone respected him for that. Everyone except Malcolm, who would never forgive Beeline for taking him away from him mother when him was six, fifteen years ago – even though him mother couldn't take care of herself, much less him. She couldn't cook, clean or sew, but she knew how to take care of her business. She was one of those women who just waited for a man to do everything for her, and when Beeline couldn't take it no more, him left with Malcolm and she found another *boops*. But Malcolm couldn't see that. All him wanted was him mother back.

I looked into my hand and I had trey-blank, six-five, six-deuce, double-five, five-deuce, and ace-blank. I looked over at Beeline and he winked at me. Behind his head, the night breeze was interfering with the shirts on the clothesline, under which Beeline's blind dog, Rass Hole, slept. Beeline called him Rass Hole so when he called him, the boss man wouldn't know if it was him or the dog Beeline was calling.

With a voice, hoarse from weed and Matterhorns, Beeline grumbled, "Natty, you pose."

I posed the double-five as a signal to him that I had at least two other pieces of five in my hand. Beeline always told me never to go down bareback in a domino game or with a woman because that would always lead to worries.

Screechy, who was standing behind me, grunted. Screechy was one of the hangers-on at the hotel, and he always held the money. Everyone trusted Screechy even though he was a mad as a bee in a cardboard box. Him wasn't mad-mad – that is, mad to hurt people and box them down. Is just when the madness lick him, him start to tell the world everybody business – who was sleeping with who wife, who was working obeah on who, who was thiefing from who. Many a marriage break up, many a politician lose them work, and many a man and woman go to jail because of Screechy's madness. But, besides Beeline, you would never find a more honest man in the district. Tonight, though, him was cool-cool, sipping on a Guinness with spliff in the corner of him mouth and watching the domino game.

Desmond, who was sitting on my left, finally broke the silence and play him trey-five and say, "Beeline, you just going take it so? Look like smady obeah you," and him turn to Murray, him partner, and say, "A really think smady must obeah Beeline because I don't think him going win this domino game."

Then Murray, trying to get Beeline riled-up, say, "It mus' be all them thing you do with you life make all this happen to you. You don't feel shame this happen to you?"

Beeline take it in stride because him did know Murray wanted him job from the time him find out that Beeline was going blind in one eye. How he found out, nobody knows because Beeline had started wearing dark glasses during the day and only took them off when him was playing dominoes. *Maybe Screechy had told him?*

Beeline laugh a bitter laugh that sound like it come from the bottom of him belly. He played double-trey, which meant that he wasn't going to break my end and that he probably had some more fives he was keeping to back me up.

"Malcolm is not me only son; me have more pickney that good. So how me must feel shame when even Papa God own pickney can turn bad and Papa God never do nothing bad? For if Papa God own pickney, who seeing him every day, can turn against him own father, then who is me to escape the judgment?"

"Is what you a talk bout Beeline?" Desmond asked, and played trey-deuce to signal to his partner that he didn't have any fives, but that he held some deuces.

"You don't know the story about Michael and Lucifer?"

"No," I said and played deuce-five because I had to test Murray with two fives. Murray passed.

The old dread smiled and shifted on the crate and took off his tam, patches of him baldhead showing through his dreadlocks. The light from the naked bulb shine on the beads of sweat that made a crown around his head.

Beeline was getting in control of the game because he had all the fives and controlled the left-hand side of the board He played five-four and I knew he was up to something. But what?

"Michael and Lucifer," he started and we know we was in for a story, which in the end we'd have to figure out, every man for himself. But that was Beeline and we were used to his stories by now.

"Papa God love Michael and Lucifer like them was him own life because them was him life. But every night Papa God turn off the light and go to sleep, next morning when him wake up, half of heaven mash up and nobody not saying nothing. And when him say, 'Who do this?' him cyaan get no answer. And him did know not to ask Michael first because him know him would only get the truth and him did want Lucifer to redeem himself."

Desmond kissed his teeth and played six-four and I came back to Beeline with six-five – my last piece of five – and Murray passed again. Beeline was in total control of the game with the rest of the fives. He played five-ace and Desmond instead of bringing his partner back into the game, put down his double-ace. I played ace-blank, Murray played deuce-blank, and Beeline laid down his double-deuce and continued with his story

"So when nobody answer after Papa God ask again, 'Who do this? Lucifer, you know anything bout this?' But the boy wouldn't answer."

"Lucifer finally say, 'No, Papa, me don't know who do this. When me get up this morning, is so me see everything stay and me say to meself, "Me don't know who would do something as wicked as this to mash up everything that you sweat so hard to make."' That was him first mistake to take Papa God for a fool."

"Then Lucifer force Papa God to ask Michael. Michael tell Papa God how everything go. Him say is Lucifer dweet."

"Papa God turn to Lucifer and say, 'Why when I ask you if is you dweet, you tell me you never know?' And him look inna the boy eye."

"And Lucifer say, 'Is not me! Is not me, Papa God! Is who you

41

going believe, me or Michael? I know you love him more than you love me. You always taking him side! You never love me!' Papa God know that wasn't true, but him never say nothing."

"And Lucifer start to bawl a sea of eye-water. And that broke Papa God heart."

Desmond played deuce-four and I played four-blank. Murray was getting mad now because he had to pass again. I knew Beeline had five-blank, which meant he could block the game. He looked around the table and counted how many cards were on the table and how many cards we had in our hands. Rass Hole came over and licked his shins.

"Papa God say, 'All right Lucifer, I will give you another chance. I going send you to a little place name Earth to do some work for me. But know this, you don't have to mash up heaven to get my attention. I will always love you, me son. I will give you another chance.' For that's how Papa God is. Him always give we, even if we bad, a second chance. Him always stand up by we side."

"And Lucifer say, 'Is punish you punishing me? Why you sending me to that likkle back-o-wall place?'"

"Papa God say, 'Start small. I have two people down there name Adam and Eve and I want you to take care of them. The two of them innocent as the day I make them. I don't want breeze to blow hard against them for them is human; them no strong like you or Michael.' For Papa God know that man is jus a breath."

"Then Lucifer say, 'You want me to baby-sit them? That sound like this is punishment. You know, all them going do is bawl all day. "Papa God I want this!" "Papa God I want that!" And is me going have to do all of that work. But I know why you giving me this!' And him flare out him wing."

"And him wait until Michael couldn't hear. 'I know you, Papa God. I see what you do when Michael not looking. I know you kill of a whole heap of people, but Michael don't know. Him only think you is good. But I know you! For is me always doing your dirty work – work that Michael would never do because him so nice and pure.' And him fold him wing."

"Papa God say, 'Son, you really think you know me? If you did really know me you would know that this is not no punishment. I love them two mud-pie on Earth with all me heart. I love them like how I love you and Michael. I will always love you and Michael. So I begging you, don't make nothing happen to them. Watch over them for me. And if you so do a good job, them will live forever.'"

"Lucifer was going caulk him ears and him say, 'Just like we?' Him couldn't believe it."

"And Papa God say, 'Jus like we.' And Lucifer fly out of there like him hear bad news."

"But just before him leave, Papa God say, 'You may leave me, but I will never leave you, my son. I will always stand by your side.' For that's how Papa God is."

From behind the kitchen where Screechy sometimes slept, a goat bleated in the darkness. Beeline played blank-six, Desmond played six-trey, and I played trey-blank. Murray was mad now like bees sting him because he passed again. Beeline looked over the game and pondered for a long time.

As him think about the game, him think bout the rest of him story. He looked out into the yard and watched how the peenie wallies circled, then swooped down into the sweet stench of the rotting guavas in the gully.

"But as soon as him leave Papa God house, it start to burn Lucifer that the dirt that used to be under him fingernail when him was helping to build Earth with Papa God was going live forever. Papa God was going mad if him did think that was going work. Dirt live forever? Madness!"

Murray was getting mad. "You going play the domino or tell story?"

Beeline didn't pay him any attention, but started to run his hands over the cards. Then he looked up at me. His fingernails were cracked and yellow as he pointed to the black spot on the dominoes and connected them to each player. He traced the game back to the beginning, matching every card each one of us had played, then he scratched the few hairs he had on his grey chin. Rass Hole whimpered and went back to sleep.

"I going finish this game and this story now. As soon as Lucifer get to earth, him start with him mischief to turn the man and him woman against Papa God, all the while thinking that Papa God would never find out if him dress himself up as a snake. And just before Papa God fall asleep, him go to the man wife and tell her a whole heap of lie, full up her head with foolishness, with him, 'Girl, you look so nice today. I could just eat you up.' She wouldn't even say, 'Is who you to be talking to me like that? Me is a married woman, go on bout you business,' cause woman like them kind of things. No, she *listen* to him. She go down by the river every day to listen to lie bout how she walk so nice and if Adam ever tell her how she walk so nice. Snake say if him was Adam him wouldn't let him woman walk bout inna the garden to make any likkle old snake come talk to *him* woman."

"And she listen to the lie and foolishness, till the snake seduce her and make her eat the fruit and when she realize what she do, she run to Adam with the lie from the snake. And poor old Adam, him did know, but him did love that likkle mawga gyal so much, for she did real pretty, that him forgive her. Instead of asking Papa God what him should do, him eat from the fruit, too, for him never want Papa God take Eve away from him. Him did love her more than him love Papa God."

"And all that happen because of Lucifer jealousy and bad mind. Bad mind and jealousy worse than obeah. So what me going do, if Papa God own son can't take the love that Papa God giving him everyday? If smady cyaan feel the love you giving them, what you going do?"

"Is true," I say, "Beeline, is true."

"Play up or shut up, old man," said Murray.

Beeline couldn't take any more and he let out a big belch that smelled like curried goat. He blocked the game with five-blank.

"I count seven with six-ace, and you, my partner, count eight with him six-deuce. I don't care how much these boys count because Murray here has double-six that I wanted to kill – that's at least twelve, and Desmond here has double-four, which is at least eight."

Desmond and Murray turned over their cards in disgust and it was just as Beeline had read the game. Murray had double-six and Desmond had double-four.

We'd won. Beeline collected the money from Screechy and got up off the crate to go down to him room. He patted Rass Hole on his head, gave me fifty dollars, and went down to the shack to kotch the door on the hinge to block the night breeze and go inside. Is then I then I figure out what him was probably going to do.

The next day, Beeline would get up early in the morning and ask Papa God what to do and if everything was irie, him would fine a lawyer, go down to the courthouse and stand up in front of the judge, not knowing what to say or how him would get the money to pay the lawyer or the bail if there was bail. Malcolm would get as much chance as him needed. All Beeline could do now was get a good night sleep, for tomorrow him was going stand up beside Malcolm and fight, the two of them, him and him son, against Babylon.

Oooh, she was going to get him. She was going to get him good. Millicent Howard clenched her teeth and felt the anger leave her jaw, travel up to her perm and down to her pedicured nails inside her Louis Vuitton shoes. She was going to get him and get him good.

While she waited after school for him to come to her classroom, she walked between her desks that were always kept in perfect order, that always matched her seating chart – which was updated every week as new students came and old students left. Every child in her care was accounted for; no one could ever blame her for neglecting a child.

The minute hand ticked upward towards three o'clock

The air conditioner went off again and she could feel the perspiration begin to trickle between her breasts, irritating the rash her doctor said had been caused by stress. And she knew why.

Her husband, Gerald, self-proclaimed "King of Real Estate in North Miami Beach", had stopped complaining about his assistant and was coming home now with stories about his new, wonderful secretary – about how fabulous she was – what a great worker she was. She knew what was coming next. Just like the last time. But she wasn't going to let her emotions get in the way like they'd done before. It had happened once too often.

She looked up at the clock and the label beside it. It was three o'clock. He was going to be late.

Millicent opened the box of pens she'd taken back from Frantz. Evidence. She always knew that behind those "Good morning, Miss Teacher" – those pathetic attempts to be courteous, there was something wrong. She had warned them all, but

46

they hadn't believed her. Now Frantz had proven her right. Now she was going to let Mrs. Barnes, the principal, and Mrs. Graves, his 'gifted' teacher, know that he was a thief.

She was going to make an example of him to all the other children who came into her class, barely speaking any English and not even trying to learn. They were getting away with murder because Mrs. Barnes and the entire administration were all afraid of being called racist. But she was going to stop that. Frantz – and all those like him – was going to feel the full fury of her wrath.

It wasn't about the flimsy box of pens. She would have given them to him if he'd asked. She bought them by the crate at the dollar store and got a tax refund on the full price.

There was a knock on the door.

Millicent said, "Come in."

Frantz entered the room and bumped a desk, shifting it out of its row. He was a minute late.

He was wearing a stained yellow shirt, dirty blue shorts, crumpled yellow socks that must have been white at some time, and a battered pair of hand-me-down shoes that were a size too small and had the sole on the left heel flapping with every step he took. And he was in the gifted programme?

She'd been poor, but she'd never been dirty. Frantz was too afraid to speak. He couldn't even say, "Good afternoon". Instead, he bowed his head and slumped into his chair. He placed his math textbook on a nearby desk.

She handed him one of the pens he'd stolen and gave him a piece of paper.

"I want you to write your mother a letter of apology for stealing the pens."

A look of horror came over the boy's face.

"And I want you to finish writing the letter before I leave at three-thirty. If you aren't finished by then, I will report this incident directly to the principal and you will be suspended. For now, if you write the letter, you might get away with just a detention. Do you understand what I'm saying?"

Frantz nodded.

"Well, get on with it!"

Now he was going to have the write the letter and she was

going to give Mrs. Barnes, Mrs. Graves, and the entire administration photocopies of his admission that he was a thief. His mother would get the original.

It was all his fault. He had to go and steal the pens from one of the gifted children who had won them as a prize for getting an "A" on her reading assignment. Then to have that little, blonde, blue-eyed girl (the last one left in the school) bawling her eyes out, because someone had stolen her pen. And Mrs. Graves had looked at Millicent with those eyes, and given her that *stare*.

The first time Millicent had seen the *stare* – the sneering contemptuous look of disregard that lumped black people into one class – she didn't understand it. She'd finally figured out what it meant when she was on a vacation in Orlando when she got into a dispute with a cashier (a frowsy little white girl she wouldn't have trusted to run a cold supper shop) at Publix Supermarket. Millicent had already calculated the amount in her head, sales tax and everything, and had her exact change, sixty-three dollars and seventy-nine cents, ready to pay the cashier. The cashier said it was eighty-nine dollars and forty-seven cents. She told Millicent that she was wrong. She said that the correct amount, according to the cash register, was eighty-nine dollars and forty-seven cents, and then she gave Millicent the stare. Millicent knew it was a malicious stare. But what did it mean, exactly?

The cashier called the manager, who looked Millicent up and down and told her that it had to be eighty-nine dollars and forty-seven cents. Millicent was counting every penny on her vacation and she wasn't going to pay for the cashier's twenty-five dollars and sixty-eight cents mistake. They rechecked every item on the list and, sure enough, when they punched the total, it was sixty-three dollars and seventy-nine cents. Millicent had been right.

But still they looked at her as if she'd done something wrong. They even had the nerve to check every single twenty, five, and dollar bill she gave them. As if they were counterfeit. They even counted the pennies. She had to endure all those stares, born from centuries of racist bile rising from their stomachs, through the lips, finally resting in their eyes, from all those white people in the store – as if she'd done something wrong. Some of them even looked as if they were going to call immigration, and then she *would* have been in the wrong. She had come to this country illegally, the one illegal thing she'd ever done in her life. But it had to be done. It was the only way.

She'd come to Miami with only seventy dollars to her name. She'd left one of the hardest ghettoes in Kingston, speaking the coarsest patois, but she'd learned to round her vowels and pronounce her "h's". She'd learned British and American English and now she was teaching English to other immigrants. She'd clawed her way up from working as a maid at the *Diplomat* on the Beach, cleaning up after white people, their toilets, their mess, their vomiting after their parties, for less than minimum wage just because she didn't have her papers. She'd married a Panamanian guy to get her a papers. She didn't see him until the divorce. Then working and going to school at nights where she met Gerald and helped him to get his real estate license. Now he was getting dressed in a separate room. No one had helped her, given her special treatment, like they were giving these children.

Back in her elementary school, Mrs. Sinclair, the worst teacher in the school, would march down the aisles with a leather strap in her right hand, scream, and point at the children with her left hand.

"Five times seven!"

She would grind her teeth as she said this.

"Tirty-five"

The child cowered.

"Six times eight!"

"Forty-eight."

The child trembled.

"Seven times nine!"

"Fifty-six?"

"Wrong!"

At that moment, the strap became transformed. It became a living thing. It wriggled through the air, abandoning its dead skin. It was almost as if Mrs. Sinclair had to grapple with its neck as it spat and hissed a spray of venomous blows over the child's arms, back, and legs – over the soft, sensitive tissues and the rough, bony cartilage around the nose and ears. The beating continued until the child became a motionless knot of flesh on the floor and then Mrs. Sinclair would continue to the eight-times tables.

Millicent never gave Mrs. Sinclair the chance to beat her – ever. She always had the right answer. She worked hard.

Donald, the boy in elementary school who she'd promised she was going to marry because he was so smart and told the funniest stories, wasn't so lucky. Mrs. Sinclair beat him until he wet his pants.

Donald never came back to school. Years later when Millicent was getting ready to leave Jamaica, tired of fighting with her mother – who always ended very quarrel with, "So, you think just because you went to high school, you're better than I am?" – she remembered Donald, the boy who had given her her first kiss under an ackee tree behind their classroom. It was hard to reconcile that memory with the picture of the half-naked man with duct tape over his mouth who had been arrested on twenty-seven counts of murder and nine counts of aggravated assault. The newspaper reported that Donald had been the enforcer of a local don, Simon "Blacka" Thompson – another of their class-mates. And *he* had graduated from one of the best high schools in Jamaica.

The minutes ticked by and the air conditioner wasn't starting up. Now she was really angry. Now Frantz was forcing her to suffer this heat with him while he was probably writing some lame excuse, some reason why he had to steal the pens. But she was ready for him. Ready for any excuse he was going to throw her way, for that was all she heard these days. Excuses, excuses.

Millicent checked her lesson plans for reading at third grade level, the envy of all her colleagues because they exceeded the county, state, and national standards for excellence.

She looked around the walls of her room. Every object was labelled so that, as the principal once said when he was presenting her with her third consecutive Teacher of the Year award, "A student only has to know the alphabet and the word 'is' and he or she could leave this room reading and speaking at least one sentence in English."

She was proud of that. She was a good teacher and she knew it. But some of these students like Frantz just weren't trying hard enough and they were making everyone look bad. All they knew were the things that they saw on MTV, the channel of black minstrels and buffoons.

Former Secretary of State, William Jennings Bryan (after whom the school had been named and whose claim to shame was to exclaim on a trip to Haiti, "Imagine! Niggers speaking French!") must have been turning in his grave, now that his all-white schools in North Miami, abandoned by white flight to Broward and Palm Beach, was being overrun with so many Haitian *pickaninnies.*

And now this! Frantz had to be taught a lesson and she was the only one who would be able to do it.

He stuck out his hand and gave her the letter he had written. It was three-fifteen.

Dear Miss Teacher

I'm sorry I took the pens sorry I did not ask I if I could borrow them to use them for something and this part is for my mom I would have to say I'm sorry for all the things I've done and caused I know you hate me I just don't belong in that kind of family but please don't beat me I just get into trouble and I always get a beating for everything I've done and I'm the most stupid one in the whole family I know you can't take it anymore so mommy you could kick me out of the house but let me pack up all my clothes and my games you could keep you could keep the animals you could sell them if you want I'll just live at my friends house and stay there forever I like you mommy and I love you always even when I die and I know you will be happy without me there

Millicent had forgotten to breathe and let out a deep sigh. One long run-on sentence. Hadn't he learned anything in her class?

"You may leave," she said and pointed to the door. "I'll see you in class tomorrow."

She brushed back her hair, which (her husband hadn't noticed) had been dyed from grey to deep auburn.

51

Frantz scurried out of the classroom.

"Don't forget your textbook!"

He ran back into the room, gathered his textbook, and dashed through the door.

Millicent folded the paper into her pocket. No one would ever see his letter.

CRY TO ME

"Hey, Professor H.," said Sean – a flash from his gold plated incisors. "Just stopping by to see how you doing. You a'ight?"

"Yeah, Sean. I'm okay."

David Hamilton brushed the pictures of Pamela, his daughter, into the open drawer. Sean had been one of the few students who'd met her when she'd stopped by during Spring Break. David didn't want Sean, whom he suspected had a crush on Pamela, to see the photos of her black eye and bruised arms.

If Sean had seen the photos, he might have tried something stupid – like beating up the boy. After all the help he'd given Sean – helping him to make bail and getting him a good lawyer for shoplifting, a minor crime as far as David was concerned – he didn't want Sean to get into any more trouble with his probation officer.

"Looking clean, Prof. H."

Sean pulled his hoodie from over his cornrows and his pants slipped midway down his thighs.

"Thanks, Sean."

It amazed David, even after all these years, the effect that tie, suit, and a regular haircut had on some of his students. But then, the only time many of his male students wore a suit was when they were going to court.

"See you around, Professor H."

"All right, Sean."

David waited until he could no longer hear Sean's footsteps lumbering down the hallway before he opened the drawer and looked again at Pam's eye.

Such beautiful eyes. Just like her mother's. Eyes that had grown even more beautiful from the time he'd first seen them in the hospital and vowed that he would always be her protector. He would never make her cry. Eyes that made him stay with her mother until she was eighteen and he figured she could take care of herself – because the thought of her crying would have broken his heart. Eyes that saved his life.

Now these eyes had been bruised by a boy he'd told her he didn't trust. When Pam had asked him why, he'd shrugged it off with, "I just don't know, Pam. Just trust me on this on this one. There's something about Ryan that's just not right."

But Pam hadn't taken his advice, and despite his objections had moved in with Ryan.

"I just love him, Daddy," she'd said. He'd held his tongue when he saw he would have hurt her if he pursued the matter any further. He guessed it was a weakness than ran in his family and there was nothing he could do about it.

Now David thought that maybe he should have told her the truth. Maybe he should have told her that before she was born, he knew how to spot men like Ryan. He had to. His life had depended on it.

But there were more pressing matters at hand. He had a mountain of essays on his desk that needed grading before he went to class later that morning. These would have to take priority over anything else he planned to do.

Reaching for one of the green felt tip pens in a coffee cup he no longer used, David took the first essay off the pile and set it on top of the calendar on his desk. He'd procrastinated long enough and couldn't afford any more excuses to put off grading this particular assignment because it was on a topic that many of his students misunderstood:

Argue for or against this proposition: "The United States of America: Protector of Democracy or Global Bully?"

The phone rang.

David almost didn't pick it up, fearing it would be one of his students requesting an extension on an essay that had been due the week before, or begging for a chance to get extra credit. Both scenarios would have resulted in the same answer. No. By now most knew better. Turn in the essay on time or get a zero. No questions asked.

But when he checked the caller ID, he saw it was from Pam's cell phone. David picked up the phone immediately.

"Pam, are you all right."

"Dad, Ryan says he misses me. He says he loves me."

"What? Why did you answer his call?"

"I didn't. He left the message on my cell. Then he kept calling and calling until I finally answered him. He says he wants to see me."

"Did you remind him about the restraining order?"

"He says he knows you put me up to it and that he knows that I love him. He says he's coming over here to see me. Daddy, I'm scared. I tried calling your cell, but it was off."

Pam began to cry.

"Don't cry, Pam. Please don't."

David waited until she stopped. In the meantime, he turned on his cell phone.

"Here's what you do, Pam. Make sure all the outside doors are locked, turn on the alarms, and go to your room. Lock that door as well."

"Should I call the police?"

"No, baby, no. Just do as I say. Please."

"Da..."

David hung up the phone and pulled his jacket from the back of his chair.

Outside in the parking lot, the air was crisp. It would have been a perfect South Florida day but for a cold snap that pushed the temperature down into the mid-forties. Even the turkey buzzards had abandoned the clear blue sky to huddle by the canals to wait for the temperature to rise so they could again follow the updrafts high above the royal palms that towered over the slow trudge of traffic.

David spotted his brand new Toyota Rav-4 parked under a banyan that had been broken by the last hurricane that breezed through South Florida. He'd always liked Toyotas from the times when he and his friends used to drive all the way from Miami in his little Corolla through the speed traps in Georgia and D.C. and into the heart of New York.

He thrust his hands inside his pocket and then reached gingerly for his keys. In his haste to leave, he'd almost forgotten that he needed to be careful on cold days like this. He had a tendency to build static electricity in his body and sometimes he'd get a mild electric jolt at times when he least expected it – opening his car door or going through his mail in the metal mailbox in the faculty office.

David climbed into the driver's seat without checking, as he usually did, for scrapes on his car. A few years ago, a student had keyed his car. David had caught him in the act. The student had almost peed himself when he saw the look on David's face. But then David had called the school security and let them handle the situation. The boy had not been worth blowing the life that he'd fought so hard to create and all that he'd tried to put behind him.

David checked his rear-view mirror and looked at his face. Did he still have the look that had so scared that student? That look that had saved him from having to give a real beatdown to so many guys who'd crossed him.

David turned the car out of the parking lot and drove quickly down a side road until he reached the ramp to the I-95.

In a few minutes, he'd be home. All the years of sacrifice had been worth it. Ten minutes away from home.

It wasn't like when he'd first started at the college and had to wake up at four o'clock in the morning to beat the traffic and get to work at seven o'clock. Now he had everything. House with manicured lawn, sprinkler system, heated pool and jacuzzi. And all in a great neighbourhood.

Indeed, he'd been surprised when one of his neighbours, who'd seen him escorting Pam inside the house after she'd gotten the beating from Ryan, asked him what had happened and said, "David, I know you're a professor and all that, but I'm Cuban and a marine. I'll kick his ass for you. He thinks he's a real man to hit a woman. But what he doesn't know is that real men don't hit women."

"I know, Cesar. I know. But I'll let the law take care of this one. But thanks."

"Anytime, David. And even if I couldn't do it, I could get someone to do it. I know people."

David thanked him again. What David didn't tell him was that he used to know people.

That he was people.

He didn't tell Cesar that back in the eighties in Jamaica, his friends used to call him "The Enforcer". It was name he'd picked up when he used to play football. His old history teacher, who'd also worked as the Caning Master and PE teacher, Coach Thompson, had noticed something in him and trained him to play sweeper – the last defender between the goal keeper and an opposing forward.

"Listen, son, from the penalty spot to this outside box," said Coach Thompson, his paunch jiggling over his thick leather belt, "if any forward invades your territory, he must pay the price. You must be willing to defend your goal like it's your mother's honour. We weren't born with claws or fangs, but we have arms and legs. Use what God gave you to stop anyone from getting to your goalie."

David became Coach Thompson's perfect protégé on what had been a losing team. The weak link was their goal keeper, Jason "Jessie" Scott or "Jezebel" as his teammates nicknamed him. Jason loved the game, but was never any good at it. The guys on his own team used to joke that Jezebel "couldn't even keep a secret." With David as sweeper, no one got near him. When David left the box to tackle a forward, they'd better pray that they were made of iron or had good health or life insurance.

David never wilfully hurt his opponents. He'd had only hurt one player really badly, but the word spread quickly through the league and few players ever challenged him. Hit one person hard enough and you could break his will and the rest of the team would collapse. Intimidation and control. That was a language his opponents understood. It worked every time.

David's reputation followed him when he left Jamaica and came to Miami on a football scholarship at a small Catholic university. He'd met up with some old football friends and they'd realized they could be making some extra money taking ganja, supplied by teammates who'd remained in Jamaica, up from

Miami to New York on the weekends – and be back in class on Monday morning.

And if after they'd made that long trip, an "associate" – as David liked to call his buyers – thought that he could get away with not paying, he'd have to have a talk with David.

"Time for some man-to-man talk," would be all David would say. The associate would have to listen to the logic of David's fists.

The last associate David had talked to had left his knuckles bloodied. The guy had buck teeth and after every punch David landed, he'd winced in pain. There was no doubt, however, who was in the greater pain. The guy never messed with their money again. From then on, all he had to do was apply what he'd learned on the football field. One look and the associate would pay.

Money was rolling in and everything was irie until the day Pam was born. David decided to stay in Miami for her birth and his friends drove into a sting set up by the police. His friends were now either dead or serving time at Rikers.

David got the news while he was holding Pam in his hands and looking into her eyes. She'd saved his life.

"Take sleep and mark death," Coach Thompson would have said.

From that day, David went back to school and found he had a knack for history. He'd graduated, won a scholarship to a state university, and went on to graduate school, stopping short of getting his doctorate only when his wife suffered a miscarriage with their second child and he needed a full-time job to support the family while she recuperated at home.

David got a job at the local community college and found that he liked teaching. When he taught history, he taught it in the same way he'd learned the discipline of enforcement from Coach Thompson, no punches pulled – not the sanitized versions that he'd got from other teachers covering up the truth about the likes of Christopher Columbus, Henry Morgan, and the butcher, Governor Eyre.

"Nations or individuals should never be afraid to use their strength," was one of Coach Thompson's favourite aphorisms. "History teaches us nothing, except that the strong dominate the weak. And it's as well they should."

David followed the lead of his former teacher. In David's classes, his students learned the facts, warts and all, about men like J. P. Morgan, Andrew Carnegie, and Henry Flagler.

Twenty years of teaching, after leaving his former life behind. Now this. Over thirty years of putting behind him those years when, as a ten-year-old boy, he saw his father beat his mother and he couldn't do a thing about it, or when he was a little older and tried to confront his father, the old man had beaten him senseless.

Years later, while David sat by his mother's hospital bed, watching her die from pancreatic cancer, he'd asked her, "Mama, why did you stay with him for all those years?"

"Because I loved him. I thought I could change him. I was waiting for him to change."

David had loved like that, but it had never done him any good. He still wondered why his wife had left him and moved back to Jamaica. He'd never laid a hand on her. He'd always respected her, even when she'd told the marriage counsellor that he had a lot of "unresolved anger issues". Challenged, she had offered no examples. He'd asked her to explain. She'd left. Why?

Maybe it was a lot of things.

Maybe it was karma as one of his students wrote in her essay about 9-11.

Maybe.

David didn't have any more time to pursue such thoughts as he turned the car down his block and noticed Ryan's car parked in the driveway. But Ryan wasn't at the front door.

David's cell phone rang.

"Dad, Dad, are you there? Come quickly. Ryan's here. He's trying to get in the back door."

"I'm here, baby. I'm here. Just lock your door and make sure that you're safe. I'll take care of this."

"What are you going to do, Daddy?"

"Don't worry yourself, Pam. Don't worry. I'm just going to talk to Ryan."

David loosened his tie and wrapped it around his fist. Ryan would never change, but after David's talk with him, he would never go near his daughter again. This time, David's knuckles weren't going to be bloodied.

FATTIE FATTIE

Kwesi Sekou woke up with a hard-on. He'd been dreaming about Rita again, though it would only lead to trouble. A man with two children, a wife, and high rent shouldn't be thinking like that. But the way Rita walked through the shop made every man feel like Donald Trump in a dollar store.

Kwesi wanted a way out of the madness, but he liked the feel of it too much. He rolled out of bed, kissed Linda on the cheek and went out to look at his back yard.

A dry August breeze blew across the rows of neatly planted tomatoes, bell-peppers, onions, thyme and other herbs. Kwesi stretched his arms over his head, and his bones cracked. Still, for thirty-eight, he wasn't in bad shape. He picked up a handful of dust and sprinkled it over an aloe that grew near the kitchen, kept there in case of burns from the fire or a pot. Squeezing juice onto the wound stopped the pain at once. Even in Miami, he'd kept a plant on the windowsill.

Since he'd come back to Jamaica, things had not gone as planned. They were living in his aunt's house, rented to him for more than he could afford, though still less than many in the neighbourhood paid. His aunt could never make up her mind if she was going to come back from Miami, but if she did, he and his family would have to leave the house. He'd been crazy to try to start over with a wife and two kids in a country he hadn't seen in fifteen years.

Yet it had been great to be back in the old neighbourhood, seeing his childhood friends, Lenny and Stewart. Lenny worked as a minibus driver; Stewart ran a small store where Kwesi sold his roots juices. It wasn't easy. Miami had confused his instincts and he had a hard time sensing things that before had been second nature.

His friends had been shocked by his dreadlocks, that he'd given up drinking and wanted to live quietly growing herbs in his backyard. Where was the Cuthbert Samuels who used to go out drinking and playing dominoes until five in the morning?

"So what really make you turn Rasta? You was trying to prove you is a real Jamaican or what?" Lenny had asked.

"Is not anything like that at all. Rasta, to me, is the only religion that tells me who I am. Is the only religion that says I and I worth anything."

"So how come your wife white?"

"She not white. She's Cuban."

"Same difference."

"Make me tell you, man. If a woman, any woman, make my heart sing, then I-man happy."

"But real Rasta don't have nothing to do with white people?"

"Real Rastas don't have to make devils out of white people."

"Is wha' kind a Rasta you is?"

"A friend of mine in Miami call me a secular Rasta."

"Wha' dat?"

Kwesi was still working that out. For him, Africa wasn't heaven and Jamaica wasn't a hellhole. Yet, Rasta had offered him something, a way of feeling like a man while he lived in the heart of Babylon.

He looked across the fence and saw Lenny cleaning his minibus. A "Quarter Million" as the kids called it – because of its price. A minibus that pretty had to cost plenty. But that was Lenny; he always had the best, no matter the price. Lenny was the luckiest man he knew. Unlike Kwesi, or especially Stewart, who never took any chances, (though he always collected on favours owed), Lenny was the daredevil of the three. He would get into all kinds of scrapes, but always walked away unscathed.

Just now, Kwesi was trying to avoid him. Sometimes Lenny said things without thinking – that was Lenny – then he'd say it was just a joke and go about his business as usual. But what he'd said about Linda really hurt.

They hadn't seen each other for about three weeks. Lenny had been away on the North Coast driving tourists between MoBay and Ochie. He took lonely women from the States on guided tours, escorting them to the most romantic and secluded spots. When he came home, rich and tired, he'd said, "Long time I don't see you, me friend. So how you and the white girl? Boy, she fat!" and smiled – and he didn't say fat like he meant good looking. He meant fat.

This was his friend. Why would he say something like that?

As he came around the corner from the yard, Linda was loading the drinks into the back of the station wagon they'd brought back from Miami. Lenny had helped him get the car through Customs. It wasn't old, but after nine months on the Jamaican roads, it was falling apart. Potholes had ruined the axles and there were rust spots on the bodywork.

Linda came towards him. Her cotton print dress, decorated with huge yellow and white flowers, was faded, and her skin was peeling from the sun and her breasts sagged like ripe jackfruits. Where was the slip of a girl he'd met fourteen years ago during his first and only year in college?

"I heard you stirring. You looked so tired I thought I'd help you."

"You shouldn't have."

He kissed her on the forehead and then tried to take the loose strand of lank hair from between his lips without her seeing.

"I'll go and see if the baby's still sleeping."

While he'd been daydreaming in the yard, Linda had loaded up all the drinks. She'd stacked them neatly in the station wagon and covered them with a crocus bag full of ice to keep them cool. It was a strenuous task, taking the crates from the kitchen, through the carport and into the car.

This was why he'd fallen so deeply in love with her – the compassion he'd seen in her care for the children at the elementary school where she'd worked as a cook and he as security. They were always the last to leave, cleaning up everyone else's mess, and from that bond, friendship, then love, had grown.

Before they moved back to the island, he'd thought it would be the big things they'd have trouble with – like a new school, new house and new neighbourhood. Instead it was little things, like not being able to get ice cream or take a shower as often as they were used to. Maybe today he'd make enough from the drinks to bring home some ice cream.

He hadn't been able to take Miami any more. The racism had got to him. Jamaica was racist too, but not in the same way. But the main reason for leaving was his children's education. They just weren't learning anything in America. When he was in primary school, he'd memorized all his times-tables by the time he was nine. In Miami they gave them calculators and computers so they didn't have to use their minds. His children would have to depend on their wits to survive, so he pulled them out.

He'd never be rich, but he could try to give his kids a good education. He could have sent them to live with his mother down in Kingston, but she had her hands full with his sister's children – wherever *she* was – but he didn't want his kids, especially his son, to grow up wild without a father – become one of those murderous teens in Miami or Kingston. Not that it couldn't happen, but the boy needed a chance.

"Dada," said Tamara, clutching a bunch of herbs from the yard, "*que es esto?*"

The sudden appearance of is daughter startled him from his reverie. He was about to scold her because she'd probably trampled a few seedlings to death. But she showed a real interest in his plants. How could he say anything hard to her when all she wanted was to learn from him?

"*Esto es una hierba para dolor del estomago.*"

"It smells *muy* nice."

Even though Linda spoke only in Spanish to her, she was beginning to lose her Spanish. He picked her up and kissed her on the cheeks. She looked so much like her mother. The same high forehead, the same wide mouth, the same beautiful smile.

"*Y donde va, Dada?*"

"*Voy a Stewart.*"

"*Quiero ir contigo.*"

"*Hoy tengo que ir solo. Comprende cielo?*"

Cielo. His heaven. That was a word he'd learned from Linda. It was a word passed from each generation of her family and now down to his daughter, though Linda's mother would never hear those words spoken to her grandchild. Before Linda's mother had met Kwesi she had joked so many times with Linda, "Anyone in our family who doesn't have a little Congo, has a little Carabali".

But then she disowned Linda for marrying a black man who'd never amount to anything. Kwesi had known they'd have trouble if he married her, but couldn't help himself. He'd fallen in love and the only reasons he could give himself for not marrying Linda were as racist as Linda's mother's.

"Okay, Dada."

Tamara ran to the kitchen, Kwesi following. Linda was breast-feeding his son, Oscar, named after her father.

"Just going," he said.

She blew him a kiss which he pretended to catch and blow back to her as he picked up the car keys off the back of the stove.

"I'll soon be back."

Kwesi put the car in reverse and eased down the driveway. He checked to see if Lenny was still home and saw Laura, his wife, backing her new Toyota Camry out of their drive. She was wearing a pink outfit Lenny had bought for her at Neiman Marcus in Miami. When they were growing up nearly every boy in Mount Airy had lusted after Laura. She was not only good-looking, but her father was one of the biggest minibus operators in Kingston. Kwesi waved to her, and she waved back. Probably on the way to the gym, keeping her girlish figure in trim.

Kwesi let her cut in front of him. He was in no hurry. He'd take his time manoeuvring around the potholes.

By the time he got to Stewart's, the freezer had already been moved to the front of the yard and Stewart was waiting for him. He straightened his tam and pointed to the crates. Stewart wore dreadlocks, though he was not a Rastaman. It was just good for business.

"You have everything?"

"The usual. Ginseng, Irish Moss, Magnum, and the crowd favourite, the Front End Lifter."

"Great, great."

Stewart paid him two hundred American dollars – a little brawta and Kwesi nodded in gratitude. Stewart patted him on the shoulder and signalled to some boys to begin unloading the crates of roots juices from the trunk.

"Last time we make good money with the Irish moss. So what make that so special?"

"Secret ingredient."

"An' you can't tell me, your brethren?"

"If I tell you it wouldn't be no secret."

There really wasn't a secret. If there was, it was where he collected the seaweed. His uncle had a small piece of land by the sea in St. Thomas where the stuff grew in large quantities. He only used what he needed and it just kept growing. He only had to harvest the stuff. After one fellow claimed it cured his impotence, his Irish moss was in high demand. Kwesi felt a little bad about this. He sold his drinks to promote good health, but knew they didn't have any ability to arouse sexual potency. That was all in the mind.

"Why you don't take a rest. Go round the front and Rita will take care of you. Me will call you when de youth finish unload the car."

This was the part of the trip that he enjoyed the most, seeing Stewart's niece, Rita. Stewart had done a favour for his sister by allowing her to live with him. His sister had complained that Rita was getting in trouble in Kingston – becoming a real leggo beast. His sister felt if they got her out of Kingston and up to Montpelier, the girl might see there was more to life than dancehalls, getting pregnant and trying to collect money from the baby fathers.

So Rita bounced around the village stirring desire in the old men who smoked outside the store and the boys of Mount Airy's soccer team who would come by to see if she was wearing the T-shirt the team captain had given her. Whenever she served Kwesi, she leant over the counter and her breasts, perky as naseberries, poked through her T-shirt.

Rita was always flirting with him and giving him playful pecks on the cheek, but the last time he'd called, she'd kissed him on the lips and that had changed everything. She was ready to take the relationship to another level, but did she think he would ever leave his wife and kids?

Yet every time he'd loaded up the station wagon, Kwesi couldn't help thinking about her, and how she'd look without the T-shirt. He'd even stopped by the store the previous evening to see her, but she wasn't there.

Kwesi sat at one of the tables outside the store. He should leave now, before things got out of control. He should leave before she came out to the table. His groin tightened.

But there was nothing wrong with just talking or sharing a few laughs, was there? Nothing wrong with that.

Hadn't King David lusted after Bathsheba and killed her husband to get her for himself? He hadn't killed anyone. Besides, hadn't King Solomon had over seven hundred wives? And wasn't he a Rastaman from the tribe of Judah from whom the sceptre would never pass? But none of this worked. *Jah, show me a way out of this madness*.

Kwesi looked over to a small playground to the right. There some kids were practising a quadrille for the summer festival. Their teachers looked on approvingly. Kwesi shook his head. Poor kids. Poor teachers. Teaching the children a dance from those people who had oppressed them for so long – bending their imaginations to fit a style that their bodies only awkwardly accepted. Why weren't they dancing their own songs, the songs that rose from their own limbs, their own bodies?

Under the awning in front of the store, a group of boys was playing marbles. The marble champion had a sock of marbles slung over his shoulder. He poured the marbles out into the dust.

"I will give you five marbles for that pretty one."

"No, is the prettiest marble me have."

"But you lose all the rest. If you swap me that marble for these five, you can get back in the game."

While the boy pondered the deal, Kwesi went inside the store, but Rita wasn't there. What was keeping her?

He looked through the window, and saw Lenny's minibus parked beside Rita's little cottage – and there was Laura's Toyota drawing up behind it.

He saw Lenny, with his trousers in his hand, scurry through the back door, jump into the mini bus and speed out of the lane. But he hit an embankment, and then a pothole and the minibus spun out on control and straight into a brick wall.

Kwesi saw Laura walk away from the cottage, ignoring whatever had happened to Lenny in the minibus, get in her car and drive away.

When Kwesi reached the Quarter Million, he saw that although Lenny was bleeding from his head, his main concern was getting his pants on. He dragged Lenny from the driver's seat, and helped him to one of the chairs outside the store.

When Stewart came around to see if he could help, Kwesi asked for some ice in a rag for Lenny's head.

"And two Appleton," he shouted.

"Him going drink two rum?" asked Stewart.

"No. One for him and one for me," said Kwesi. "Him need it more than me, but him shouldn't drink alone."

"I thought you'd given up drinking because of your vows to God," said Stewart.

"God should never come between two brethren," said Kwesi. "When you brethren in trouble, everything goes out the window. Jah will forgive I for this, for Jah is bigger than any thought I could have."

Stewart brought the rag with the ice and put the drinks on the table.

Kwesi put the rag on Lenny's head. He took a sip of the drink and tasted the cool fire in the rum. It had been seven years since he'd had a drink. He stretched out his legs and clinked the ice in his drink.

The boys had gone back to their game of marbles.

"Okay, I will swap. But for ten marbles."

The marble champion smiled and doled out ten marbles and slipped the prized marble into his pouch with the other marbles.

"Doan do that! You'll chip it."

"Is mine now. I can do anything I want with it."

"I'll swap it back right now."

"Too late. The deal done. You have to play."

"I can't believe it," said Lenny. "I can't believe it."

"So why you do it?" asked Kwesi. "You had everything! The prettiest and the richest girl in Mount Airy. A nice family, pretty daughter. The Quarter Million."

"Pretty girl, pretty daughter, the quarter million," said Lenny, and turned his head away. "Laura don't come near me in the past year. She always telling me how she have a pain in her belly when the only place I know she go is the gym and beauty parlour. As for my daughter, she poison that little girl mind against me. Man, I am a stranger in me own house. Man, you so lucky you have a wife like Linda. I see her, I see her this morning while you was kotching in the yard. That woman lift all them crate into you car while you was resting. Who is the lucky one?"

Kwesi took another sip of his drink, and almost spat it out. He hadn't missed this life. He sat silently and listened to Lenny pour out his troubles.

"As far as her father concern, she give him a granddaughter, so the line can continue. Him going probably take her back now."

"What you going do now?"

"Live. That's all me can do now," said Lenny.

Stewart came inside and told them the police were outside. Kwesi got up to help Lenny, but Stewart held his hand.

"Make me take care of this one," said Stewart.

"How much for the drinks?"

"You don't think him pay enough all ready," Stewart said. Kwesi nodded.

Lenny walked outside and saw the police peering at the minibus. With Stewart's help he could probably get off any charges. But that was all. Lenny would owe him big time.

"You know," said Stewart to Kwesi, "I could see this coming."

"How?"

"Every time she take up with another married man, she find some boops who thinks love is anytime him hood get stiff. Never think Lenny would be a boops."

Boops. He remembered that word.

Kwesi looked around the yard. Across the street, the dancers were still practising their quadrille. Rita came back to the store and smiled at him. She had on a new T-shirt. Kwesi ignored her.

Going out to the car, he saw that the boy had won back his prized marble, and guessed from his face he wouldn't be taking any more chances.

Kwesi checked his rear-view mirror, and saw Lenny stumble on Stewart's shoulder. He put the car in first gear. He had to stop daydreaming. Jah had shown him the way. He was going home to make love to his fat wife.

JOSEPH'S DREAM

A pelican circled Biscayne Bay above the tops of the buoys that rocked gently in the ebb of the tide pulling away from the shore. The sea mirrored the stillness of the palms, and a few windsurfers, camped near fists of mangroves that sprouted along the coast, were waiting for a gust of wind to take them out to sea.

Joseph Forrester turned away from the window to look back at the spot on Silvio's office door where the nameplate had been removed, now only a rectangle a shade darker than the rest of the door.

"Silvio always said that they're out there circling, ' he said to Betty, his secretary. "Ready for your first stumble to take you down."

★

Joseph's company, KinderLove had been born on napkins at *El Paradiso*, a small Cuban restaurant on South Beach. Joseph had been having lunch with Silvio, who'd introduced him to the restaurant – the only place in Miami where you could get authentic Cuban food – like the food from Oriente, the province where Silvio had been born.

Silvio had left Cuba when he was ten but still had vivid memories of the town where he grew up. He dreamed of going back, but for now it was the restaurant that had to assuage his homesickness.

Joseph loved the food there. He'd told Silvio that he must have been part Cuban the way he felt about the *arroz con pollo,* and that the only thing that separated them was their accents.

"We all came on one ship," said Silvio, "But sometimes we forget."

"You think you could actually make money in this business?"

"No one's taking care of the children any more. We're all working two, three jobs and it's not like our homelands where you had grandma or a cousin to watch over the kids. But you have to be careful."

"How?"

"Well," said Silvio, "noncompliance over things such as cock-roaches, or the staff-child ratio can get you into trouble, but big things, like even a hint of child abuse, especially after Wacko Jacko, or any hint of sexual scandal and you're history. HRS doesn't take kindly to that kind of stuff."

"So why was your wife's place closed?" Joseph asked.

"The play areas were too small."

"Too small! You're kidding, right? I've been there with you; those play grounds were huge!"

"But the owner decided to take in some more children which prompted a review. HRS came and remeasured the play area and they said it was not up to code. Until it was, they had to shut down. The owner couldn't afford the rebuilding, so they closed."

"Just for that?"

"Just for that. The owner figures a former employee was out to get her. Probably the girl she'd fired for bringing in a copy of *Playgirl* and reading it while the kids were sleeping. None of the kids saw it, but when it was reported to the owner, she had to fire the girl. She didn't want to take any chances.

"Interesting."

"So are you ready to make some money, my friend?"

"Any time you are, *hermano*."

It was then that Joseph began laying out the groundwork for the company that he had always dreamt would show everyone from Mount Airy what he could do.

When his mother died, leaving him only his name, he ran away from home, vowing he'd never go back to the island until he could show everyone how successful he'd become – without their help. Everyone in Mount Airy thought he was mad. How would an eighteen year old boy survive in America? But he did. He courted an American college girl, married and divorced her to get his papers, and then he was free to get any job he wanted.

First, he'd worked as a security guard to build his credit, and then as a telemarketer for the quick cash. After that, community college and working as a bank teller in Hollywood Federal, then Southeast Bank, where he'd worked as a loan officer and met Silvio when he handled a loan to refinance Silvio's home. After leaving Southeast, he'd moved to Argo Savings and Loan, and risen from senior loans officer to vice president. But then, after a series of bad loans, the company had been faced with bankruptcy, been taken over by the government and sold to another banking conglomerate.

Things had started going badly for Joseph when a local television station did a story on the bank which implied that he was tied up in the scandal of the bad loans. The newspapers joined in, and the customers had clamoured for their money. That was when everything had gone belly-up. Although Joseph hadn't been responsible for the bad loans, his reputation had been tarnished. All he could do was cut out a picture of the television reporter, Ray Santiago, who'd started the trouble, and throw darts at it.

Joseph began by making a list of all the people whom he thought would be helpful. Then he went to the library and local chamber of commerce and combed through all the statutes regarding childcare centers. He hired his friend, Jerry Bucher, on a retainer – it was always perfectly clear for Joseph where friendship ended and business began – and had him draw up all the legal agreements. Jerry had worked in the legal department at Argo. With Jerry he'd searched through all the public records and newspapers for childcare centers that were in trouble.

Joseph's strategy was to approach the owners of the childcare centers with a deal. For a percentage of the ownership, he would broker a loan using his capital and part of the money he had received for his early retirement, bring in a team of architects and builders, and restructure the centers to the dimensions which met the State's standards.

Once he had secured enough businesses through partnerships of this kind, it was time to begin building childcare centers of his own. It was then that he called in Silvio. If his wife Noemi was named as a co-owner and president of the company, they could secure minority contracts and loans through Small Business Administration. He didn't want to put his name down as the owner. Because of his reputation, the banks would be reluctant to lend him money, but he could invest as a silent partner. This was how Silvio could help

At first, Silvio didn't want any part of it, and Joseph had to make it lucrative for him to leave his job as a Dade county schoolteacher. There were other conditions.

"I don't want any part of it, if it involves any deception. You know, people look at us Cubans, in fact, all Latinos, and they think we're all corrupt. They say it was corruption under Batista that led to Fidel's coming to power and it's the same corruption that's going to lead to his fall. Well, if that's true, then this is one Cuban who wants to make sure that when Fidel falls, there will be no more corruption in Cuba. When my family left Cuba, we did not leave our dignity behind."

"So how do you think I feel? All Jamaicans are drug dealers! That's why I have to be in the background."

Joseph had heard Silvio's speech before, but he knew his friend was serious. Silvio was proud of his family name, Montoya. Joseph remembered their first meeting, when his bank was trying to open a new branch in Hialeah. They were having a difficult time attracting clients because the bank was perceived in the Cuban community as being prejudiced against them.

Joseph had come up with a campaign to run during Hispanic Heritage Month which featured Cuban writers and artists. With the investment the bank was making in the programme, they needed someone they could trust who was respected within the Cuban community. Silvio was nominated by his school board to oversee the project.

After several meetings, Joseph realized they had common interests in tennis and golf, and they began playing together at charity events in Miami. It was after one of these tournaments that Silvio had told him about the significance of his name.

His great grandfather had come from Madrid, and once been part of the nobility in Spain. Several members of his family had fought during the Spanish American War – on both sides. They had fought against Fidel when he came to power. Their name, though now forgotten in the history of Cuba, had always stood for honour and bravery. "I would never sully my family name for any momentary financial reward," Silvio had declared.

"I hear you, Silvio. It's how I feel about those kids who are wearing their pants around their ankles and practising the jail house shuffle."

"I'll tell what's worse, Joseph. My countrymen who have thrown off their names. Traded Francisco for Frank, and Jose for Joe. How could the grandeur of a name like Francisco be traded for a bland name like Frank?"

Joseph had listened to Silvio's story as he had listened to all the other stories he'd heard about Cuba. He was sceptical. All the Cubans he'd ever met claimed to have had tons of money in Cuba. For them the air was cleaner, the fruits sweeter, and the women prettier: a paradise. At first, he dismissed it all as the mere ranting of exiles.

But Silvio was different. He'd never claimed to have had money, just his name.

"Still," said Joseph. "you're making it sound worse than it really is. Think about Harvey's and Goldstein."

"Harvey's and Goldstein. I bought some shoes there last Christmas. They can change their names, but I can't change my skin."

"They've started taking over on Miami Beach. But can you see anyone on the Beach walking into a shoe store named Salazar and Gonzalez Shoe Store?"

"I see."

"Those guys were smart," said Joseph. "They saw an opportunity and they grabbed it, and that's what we've got to do."

"And it was all on the up and up?"

"Only a name change. And hell, people do that every day in Miami. We might even change your name to Sam Martin."

Joseph waited for the look of surprise on Silvio's face before he smiled knowingly, "I know, Silvio, I know."

Silvio smiled. Joseph had put one over on him.

"Where do I sign?" Silvio said, and they shook hands. He couldn't wait to get home to tell Noemi the good news. In his mind, he composed his letter of resignation to his school. He wanted to give them as much time as possible to find a replacement.

With Noemi as the nominal president of KinderLove Day Care Center, Joseph moved into offices overlooking the bay. Silvio put his nameplate on the door, repeating his mantra about how a man's name was his trust, his honour. He had also managed to recruit several other teachers who already had HRS clearance and FBI checks. He didn't want the centers to be merely warehouses for children; they had to give quality education. This had been one of Silvio's main demands. It was he who suggested changing the name to KinderLove Child Care Center.

Joseph asked. "Why?"

"To stress that we take care of children, not days."

"That's smart. I'll make a real capitalist of you yet," said Joseph.

"And I'll make a father of you yet. When are you going to settle down? What's the use of having all this money if you don't have a family to share it with? When are you going to get yourself a son to leave your empire to?"

"Son? What would I do with a kid?"

"Teach him."

"Teach him? What do I know?"

"A lot more than you think, my friend. A lot more.'

After that, Joseph opened other childcare centers in low-income areas like Alapattah, Liberty City, and Little Haiti, using the same methods he had used with Silvio. By this time, however, he had enough capital to buy the land, and build the center to the highest specifications. All he needed was a plot of land, and he could build a replica of his center, put his people in place, and move on. He had enough money now to finance his building programme and no longer needed Silvio's and Noemi's minority status to finance his loans. He paid Silvio for his share of the business.

Silvio continued to be a manager, for he was committed to the project. It was doing well. Mothers, who before had stayed at home and collected welfare checks, were now leaving their children in the child care center, and through a deal Joseph had made with the community college, they were getting financial help to enrol for college courses.

"Hell, we could become the McDonald's of childcare centers in Miami. Over one billion children served," he joked with Silvio.

Soon Joseph had nine day care centers in three counties, all headed by the right people, as he saw it. He had black managers in Liberty City, Haitian managers in Little Haiti and Jewish managers on Miami Beach – they were all a part of the KinderLove family.

He envisioned a steady progress up the Gold Coast and across the state to Tampa, building his company by selecting each manager according to the racial composition of the area.

"Can you imagine," he said to Silvio, "once Cuba opens up we could set up centers there. With everybody going back to rebuild, they'll need someone to take care of their children. Hell, I might put you in charge of all my Cuban operations."

Silvio thought that Joseph was joking, but he wasn't. Once the island became free again, Silvio would be an excellent choice to run operations in Cuba. He really kept a tight watch on all expenditure and daily operations. Once he reprimanded a secretary, a fellow Cuban, for taking pencils home for her son.

"Relax, it's only a box of pencils," said Joseph.

"It starts with pencils," Silvio said . "I'm not going to see the Hialeah center destroyed by theft.

Silvio built the Hialeah Branch up from nothing. It was a tough sell because most families preferred to leave the children with their *abuelas,* but Silvio challenged them: "Do you think *abuela* can help your children when all the other American children are all working on computers and cell phones and we're still playing *bolitas*?"

Soon the center was filled with children from all over Hialeah. At that time, Joseph was opening a new branch in West Palm Beach and he needed Silvio to jumpstart the project. Silvio needed help, so he did something he'd never done before. He hired someone from his family.

"And you're sure Caridad is okay," he'd asked his cousin Rodrigo.

"She's okay, man. She's had a small problem in the past with a professor at UM, but everything worked out. She's changed. She graduated with honours in education and computer science. She's just the person you're looking for."

"What kind of trouble was she in?"

"Nothing big. Something about her grades. It was nothing. You know these Americans; they're always making something out of nothing."

Noemi suggested that Silvio should invite her to dinner. Afterwards he watched Caridad mingle with the guests and show off her breadth of knowledge about current affairs and history. She was a model of Cuban-American grace and charm, fluent in both English and Spanish, and not the Spanglish they spoke on Calle Ocho, but something approaching Castilian Spanish. She loved children and she would have gone into teaching if the salary had been better. Instead she'd gone into computer science. Silvio decided to hire her.

From the start he was impressed. She was tall, blond, and green-eyed, but she never allowed her good looks to interfere with her professional behaviour. She was a model of the new Latin woman – with enough of the old ways to charm and enough of the new ways to impress with her competence.

Joseph was awed with her credentials and showed her off at various events around Miami. She ran the Hialeah center without a hitch. Fathers would spend hours trying to get interviews with her regarding the progress of their children and would spread the word about how cooperative she was. Mothers were impressed by her interest in their families. She was perfect. Then Silvio found something in the files and reported it to Joseph.

"What's up Silvio? More missing pencils?"

"This is a lot worse. Take a look at this."

Silvio placed a file from the Hialeah office on Joseph's desk. There were requisitions for toys, vacation leave, invoices for food, pay stubs and HRS maintenance forms and licenses. Joseph looked over the files; everything seemed to be in order.

"What's the problem, Silvio? Everything looks okay to me."

"Everything," said Silvio, "except this request for leave which I didn't sign."

"You didn't? There's your signature."

"It isn't mine. She forged my signature, Joseph."

"Forgery. That's a serious charge. When you get to the bottom of this, tell me what I should do. She's your girl."

The last sentence stung Silvio, but he didn't say anything

because it was true. He'd hired Caridad. Now she had put him in a bind; he had to be tough with her, extra tough. It was a matter of principle. If word got out that he'd been soft on her, then morale in the whole company would go down.

"She's done everything by the book until today," said Silvio. "But we have to let her go. The word has probably spread all around the company. We've got to do something."

"We've got to move carefully, though," said Joseph. "Let me handle this."

"Are you sure?"

"Things like this can break up a family and the last thing that I want is for your family to suffer. My family broke apart over something much smaller than this and we've never forgiven each other."

"KinderLove is a company, Joseph. It's not a family."

"For me it is."

Joseph waited until Silvio was away from Miami before asking Caridad to come down to the main office.

"But, why?" she protested. "Haven't I worked and worked for this company giving it a hundred and ten percent all the time. I've even worked weekends without charging anyone. I worked on the payroll and everything else including the typing and correspondence when my secretary was out. I did all the work in the branch, and because I took two weeks, you're going to fire me?'

"All you had to do was ask, and you would have gotten it. It was all yours for the taking."

"You mean because I took two weeks..."

"It was on company time, and you forged Silvio's signature. That was wrong."

"And you've never done anything wrong in your life?"

"Not like this. You've disappointed Silvio and your family. Your name."

She stared at him and then began to cry.

Joseph tried to comfort her, but she would have nothing to do with him. Joseph told her he would write a letter of recommendation for her, and wouldn't mention why she'd left KinderLove. Everything would remain between them and nobody else would need to know about the affair. He spent an hour trying to console her. But when she came out she still looked so shaken that Joseph's secretary, Betty, (who had never trusted Caridad) had asked, "What's wrong, Miss Caridad?"

"Nothing, nothing at all," snapped Caridad. "I just want you to record the time that I went into that man's office and record the time that I left," she sobbed. "That beast!" she screamed as she ran down the hallway.

Joseph came to the door when he heard her scream. He thought she'd taken it badly, but not like this. As he was about to go into his office, Betty mumbled something under her breath.

"Sorry for mawga dawg, mawga dawg turn round and bite you."

"What?" She was always coming up with these quaint island sayings when she needed to make her point obliquely.

"Don't worry yourself, Mr. Joseph. You'll see her again," said Betty. "Girls like that always land on their backs."

She was right. Caridad came back, but not in the way he had expected. She rallied the parents to her side, and many signed petitions demanding her reinstatement.

When Silvio tried to stand up for Joseph, voices in the local Cuban media branded him a communist and a traitor to his race. Caridad's uncle came on a Cuban radio station claiming that Silvio's family had been supporters of Fidel; an *El Nuevo Herald* editorial denounced the racial hiring practices of KinderLove Inc. and Ray Santiago joined in with regular *exposés* of KinderLove.

At this point, Joseph started to get worried, but Silvio reassured him that it would soon die down. People would soon see through Caridad's tricks.

"We can reveal what she did, and the reasons we fired her," Silvio said. "She's saying that I was the one who authorized everything and that I'm afraid of you."

"Don't say anything," said Joseph. "You'll just make matters worse. This is between her and me."

A week passed and the picketing continued. Silvio tried calling Caridad, but she directed him to her lawyers. Joseph was losing business in Hialeah – though picking up some trade in Palm Beach. He had to act. He called Silvio into his office, and told him about his plan.

"I'm reassigning you to Monroe County, Silvio. And I'm bringing back Caridad to Hialeah. I'm sorry, but I have to do this."

"But that's almost admitting that you've done something wrong. She has shamed me, my family."

"I have to do it for the sake of the business. It's the only way I can get your people off my back."

The words "your people" had never hurt Silvio so much.

"They're not my people when they behave like that!"

"They are now, and they want your blood."

Silvio was stunned. He leaned back in his chair and watched the pelicans dive into the sea. Along the shore some kids were collecting shells on the beach.

"I can't do it, Joseph. I can't live under a cloud."

"What are you saying?"

"I have to leave."

"Why?"

"It's better that I leave with a good conscience so I can live with myself. Do what you have to do."

"Suit yourself, *amigo*, suit yourself," said Joseph. "I'm not going to beg."

Joseph almost choked on the words, but this was business and he was not ready to drown. Silvio would have to sink or swim on his own.

Joseph figured he would call the girl into his office, give her a few drinks, and offer her old job back with a raise; perhaps give her Silvio's office. All this seemed to him to be quite reasonable, and he was sure Caridad would accept. He'd always had the feeling she was not the demure Cuban girl everyone was making her out to be. Both of them would be satisfied. She would have her old job back, and he would be rid of all the bad press.

When Silvio packed up, he'd been careful to take only the things he'd purchased with his own money for his office. Although it was unnecessary, he'd composed a letter of resignation. It was hard leaving the office where he had so many fond memories, but the really hard part had been breaking the news to his wife.

How was he going to tell her, after all they'd been through, that he was out of a job? How were they going to face the future without the health insurance or any of the others benefits the job had provided? He'd saved some money; always put aside something each month, but what if something really catastrophic happened? What would he do?

On the long drive home on the I-95, Silvio had looked across the Julia Tuttle Causeway and he realized how much Hurricane Wilma had changed Miami. For six years, even through the hurricane, he had gone to work at six and often reached home after ten at night. He hadn't realized how many trees had disappeared from the skyline.

When he got home, he'd told his wife and children the bad news. They'd have to cut back on a few things. The kids would probably be taking lunch to school, and they might have to give up the cable television. The children started crying.

Later that night, after she'd tucked in the kids, Noemi told him that she'd explained the situation to them and she would take a second job to help out.

"But you're already working too hard. The kids need one of us to be around."

"Don't worry. Now that you're out of a job, you'll have lots of free time on your hands."

He'd marvelled how she could always make light out of things that seemed to him to be so difficult. But this was why he had married her.

When he woke up next day, Silvio began updating his resume. He searched through the newspapers and contacted old friends. Six weeks passed before he was invited for his first interview. It was downtown, so he decided to visit his old office to pick up the rest of this things, and to say hello to his former co-workers.

When he got to the office, Joseph's door was shut, but when Betty saw him, she greeted him with a hug and a kiss on his cheek. Silvio was surprised, he had never seen her so expressive.

"You is a good man. Take care of yourself," she said.

"Where's Joseph?"

"He inside the office with the lawyer. He had a meeting with the girl and she pulled a new stunt with him, but this time in broad daylight – and he wanted to give her your job!"

"Did she take it?"

"Bigger dumplings to fry!"

"What? Please, Betty don't go into your Jamaican now when I need the facts."

Betty explained that Caridad had been offered a new job with a raise, but she wanted everything in writing.

"Did he give it to her?"

"Of course. That girl have that man wrap around her finger like a dog looking for him shadow. The fool give her everything she wanted, just to stop them people from coming around here."

She saw the look on Silvio's face. "You know what I mean, sir?"

"I know, Betty. I know"

"The next day the girl file a complaint with the Equal Opportunity people, and before you know it them was all over the office. But don't worry, you not involved."

Silvio wanted to stay, but he realized he had to get to his interview, and he didn't want to be late. He picked up the box with the rest of his things Betty had packed for him. Before he headed out, he pried his nameplate off the door and put it in his box.

"I don't think anyone will mind if I take this."

"I don't think so," said Betty. "And what him can do, fire you?"

Silvio smiled. "Tell the boss I stopped by," he said as he walked past Joseph's door, which opened at that moment. Jerry Bucher, Joseph's lawyer, stepped into the hallway. Seeing Silvio, he stepped back and closed the door in his face.

Joseph had seen Silvio and he asked, "What did you do that for?"

"He may be in this with her. You never know these Cubans."

Joseph was about to scold Jerry, but he didn't.

"So there's nothing we can do?"

"Nothing. She's got you by the short ones, Joseph. We gotta just pay and move on. She's an attractive woman. You're a bachelor. You don't have any family ties, a loyal wife, or kids to stand beside you on these charges of sexual harassment."

"This almost ruins me."

"You have no option, Joseph. And now Silvio is out, if she wants to play the anti-Cuban card, you're dead."

"If she wants..."

"If she wants.... She's a real pro at this stuff. I've checked around and she did this with one of her professors at UM. They settled out of court, of course. But that was for chicken feed and good grades. This is big time and you're it."

"I'm it?"

"You're it! I'll see you tomorrow with the papers.

Joseph followed him out of his office into the reception area and stood looking out of the window. The pelican plunged into the water, hungry for food.

HOW DO YOU TELL?

How do you tell your parents that you know you are a Russian? That you've known this all your life, and that you're no longer afraid to tell everyone who you really are. How do you? If you're a girl and you tell your mother, she'll cry and say, "Don't breathe a word to your father. He'll never understand. Just fake everything, like I've done in my own way, for the past sixteen years."

And if you're a boy, you better not tell your father until after your twenty-first birthday and you're far away from home. For he survived the MAD times and will surely beat the Russian out of you. For when you tell him, he will suddenly see his future, like a road stretching into infinity, taking a detour to a dead end. He'll say that the Russianness must come from your mother's side of the family because no one in his family is a Russian. And if you try and comfort him by saying something like, "It's a new millennium, Dad. It's not like the old days when Russians were brought up before courts or Congress for undermining the American Way. Russians can get married and in some parts of America they can even adopt children." That's when he will rant and rave because he's a cold-war warrior who still believes in traditional family values, and it's always these Russians (there are so many now) who have corrupted every single American value and now they want to get married and adopt children? Impossible!

He may even accuse you of being a terrorist and trying to subvert the American family. He knows Russians will never be true Americans. He'll then call in the local pastor to counsel you out of your Russian lifestyle – which he knows is only a passing phase. The pastor will pray for you, suggest fasting, exorcism, intervention therapy or hormone treatment and show you videos of other Russians, their faces beaming with joy, who have converted from this un-American way of life, given up the Russian fad, and now they've bought a vacation home in North Carolina, have a family with two children a dog and a cat, are proud Rotarians and drive SUVs. Who could want anything more?

But how do you keep a secret that's entwined in the double helix of your DNA? And who would you tell? Would you have to go walking the malls, boulevards, or, when you're older, go to a neighbourhood bar looking for another Russian (always with the fear in your chest someone will remember the Wall and kill you because you're a Russian) who's drinking vodka, straight up, no chaser?

Or do you meet at night with other Russians in secret cells, exchanging secret handshakes and war stories, shedding the fictions of your other lives like loosely worn garments, and always remembering the slogans from the good old days before you were forced underground: "Russians of the World, Unite!"

No, you'll keep the secret to yourself and never tell a soul. For how do you know that the person you've met at the local bar is really a Russian like you and not a double agent, a spy for the other side? Until one day, out of sheer loneliness and despair, you'll drop your guard and say, "To hell with it! Today, if it comes to that, I'll die as myself," and sidle up to the stranger at the far end of the bar who's still smoking Marlboros in defiance of the law. And as you get closer, you will always wonder, just at the point of meeting, whether this could mean the end of your life. Is this the beginning of love or a trap?

COWARD MEN KEEP SOUND BONES

Randall Edwards had always been a cautious man. During the last year of his six years of marriage to Angela, whenever he went out with his friend, Wallace, on a Friday night, and turned to the girls from the *Palace* on 79th and Biscayne, he would only get hand jobs, or if she was really cute and he'd checked her gums, he would allow her to give him a blow job. When he came home to Angela, he'd make sure that he'd bathed and washed properly before slipping under the comforter – before she moved away from him.

Six months after the final settlement of the divorce, on the Friday before the Labor Day weekend, Wallace slurred over a frothy mug of Bud, "Man, you would never believe who I saw last week."

"Who?"

"Desiree Marshall."

Randall placed his mug on the counter and wiped his lips on a clean napkin.

"You're lying. You're lying, bro."

"I ain't lying, man. I ain't lying. And you won't believe where."

No doubt at the Aventura Mall or downtown in the Government Center. Maybe Wallace had gotten her number, so he could look her up.

"Where?"

"Down by the back of the *Black Madonna*."

"Now I know you're lying."

"If I'm lying, you're buying. And I've never lost a bet."

Randall and Wallace had been friends from the early days of high school where they'd learned how to design software for vidco games, and a chess club, where they'd led their team to three consecutive victories over the rich kids from Coral Gables. They'd given the trophy to Mr. Reid, the principal, because he was the first to recognize their talent. In turn, he'd bought them T-shirts with their names across the back. For a brief moment, they were nearly as popular as the guys on the football team and not just those "Black Geeks".

Randall had given Desiree his T-shirt. She'd worn it to school every day since they'd won the state championship and he was planning to ask her out on a date or even get a kiss. They continued smiling and talking to each other at lunch and he walked with her home after school. She'd even touched his hand one afternoon when he left her by her gate. Randall couldn't have been happier.

Then one day Desiree handed the T-shirt back to him. The next thing he knew, Angela, the most popular girl in the school and the principal's niece, was kissing him in front of Desiree and the whole class – which made them a couple. Everything happened quickly after that.

He learned that Desiree was seeing another boy and that they were going to get married after graduation. Randall would have been depressed if Angela hadn't invited him over to her house one Friday night when her parents were out. Looking back, he realized Angela had seduced him. It was his first time with a girl and she was always willing. He had sex with Angela four times a week while her mother worked as a private nurse for some rich white people on La Gorse Island. Life was sweet.

When Randall and Wallace graduated, they were offered jobs to train with Xymax to design software. Their starting salary was thirty thousand a year and by the time he'd left they were making seventy thousand. Before Randall knew it, he was married to Angela who, until she found her vocation as a consultant for a loan company, stayed at home and took classes at a Biscayne College.

"We've done it," he'd said to Wallace one night at the *Rusty Pelican* as they sipped Dom Perignon and looked at the Miami skyline.

"Look at us! A Jamaican and a Bahamian, no fathers, no family, but we did it!"

They were survivors. They'd had done it all without support from their families. Randall's mother had left his father when he was three, and he'd been brought up by his father and several "aunts".

But then, after six good years, Xymax crashed with the other dotcoms. Angela moved out and went to Texas. Randall remained in South Florida. Through it all, Wallace had stuck by him and got him a job at his college. Then they started drinking together. They'd started at sports bars, then nightclubs and strip clubs, from one dingy bar to the next. There were no new prospects on the horizon and fixing computers at the college wasn't cutting it. *Exiles* was the only bar where Randall and Wallace could drink without fear of being recognized by the kids from Biscayne College.

"I know it can't be her. I know you're lying."

"Come with me and you'll see."

Randall gulped down the remainder of his beer and ran after Wallace. As they drove through the streets of Liberty City, Randall wondered how Desiree had come to this. When they were in high school, "luminous" was the only word that could describe her. He and his cousins used to walk by her house every day on the way to school, even though it was out of their way.

Randall thought Wallace was lost as they kept circling round Little Haiti and back to Liberty City until he spotted a group of hookers hanging out behind *Club Nouveau*. Then he saw Desiree. She was high. He could see it in they way she staggered up the street. But when she stopped and steadied herself, he could see a remnant of the old, dignified pride that made her stand out from the rest of the girls with names like Sheniqua, Raywanda, and Tirabella. He remembered the touch of her hand on his. Maybe he would allow her to give him a blow job.

With the lights of the car turned off, Wallace coasted up to the sidewalk where hookers had already unbuttoned their blouses and were baring their breasts. Desiree walked up to the car and tapped on the window. Randall rolled it down.

"Back for more, eh. I sucked you off real good the last time, didn't I. Real good. I told you I could suck the cork out of a wine bottle."

Wallace turned to Randall and gave him a sheepish look, but Randall didn't care. Ten years ago, it would have mattered.

Desiree's eyes focused and when she saw Randall in the passenger seat, she backed away, but when Wallace shook a bag of rocks in front of her, she knocked on the back window again and Wallace unlocked the door.

"Let's go," she said as she piled into the back seat to the cheers of the other hookers.

Wallace turned on the lights and peeled away from the corner. He did a u-turn on Biscayne Boulevard, and headed for the *Vagabond Hotel*. He could have done it in the car like the last time or gone back to her place, but he knew Randall only too well, so he paid for the room.

"I'll go first, cause, like I said, if I'm lying, you're paying."

Randall nodded. It didn't matter

As Wallace walked up the stairs with Desiree he passed her the rocks. Randall watched from the car.

He watched the lights go on and Wallace's shadow bounce against the window, sometimes tall, sometimes short. After about five minutes, Randall came out of the hotel smiling and zipping up his fly.

"She's all yours, bro. You can pay me later."

Randall hesitated. It wasn't the first time he'd been with a hooker since his marriage fell apart, but was this was Desiree. He climbed the stairs.

When he opened the door, he glanced over at the lamp on the scuffed night table, with plastic flowers and a condom beside a brown ashtray. Desiree was wearing a red teddy. Stretch marks curved around her waist and stomach down into a mass of pubic hair.

He had dreamed about something very different from this all through high school. Now her hair was tangled and she had dark circles under her eyes. But her face was still beautiful. Despite the years of abuse, her cheeks still had a copper glow and the long black hair she had inherited from her Seminole grandmother rested in a clump on her shoulders.

"So, how much do I owe you."

Desiree began to cry. She patted the bed for him to sit beside her, but he refused until she looked up at him with her beautiful black eyes. Randall sat beside her and held her shoulders. She sobbed on his chest. This was the closest he had ever come in contact with a hooker's bodily fluids.

"What happened, Desiree?"

She cried for another ten minutes before the words came out. Desiree told him that when her mother died she didn't have a home, so she'd moved in with an uncle. For a price. It started out with a little weed, then crack and when he died from AIDS, she was out on her own.

"I mean between us in high school?"

"You mean you still don't know?"

"What?"

"Angela told me that you were a couple and that I was trying to steal her man. When she came up and kissed you in front of me, I knew she was right and that you were playing me. Why did you do that, Randall? I didn't deserve that. I didn't deserve that. Not from you."

"Why did you give me back the T-shirt?"

"What was I supposed to do? Keep on wearing it when you belonged to another girl? I ain't no fool, Randall."

Randall was about to get up from the bed, but Desiree held him down and began unzipping his pants.

"No, I can't do this. Not now."

"Wallace promised me more rocks if I did this."

The beers had got the better of him and Desiree was determined. She pulled out his penis and as he looked down to see her lips, he exploded in her mouth.

"Damn, you were quick. A hundred dollars your friend told me. He wasn't paying for time, just work."

Randall threw five twenties on the bed. It was too much, but he didn't care. He just wanted to be out of the room.

As he got into the passenger's seat, he looked up at the lights in the hotel room.

"Man. You must have fucked her real good. Did you use the helmet I left for you on the table? You must have been a stallion, bro. Finally got that puss you always wanted. Damn, bro, I always told you you were the lucky one."

'Yeah."

He wasn't angry with Wallace; he meant well. He had left him a condom after all.

As Wallace headed straight for the I-95, the buildings and the lights of Miami blurred by the window. Randall looked at his hands. When he slipped alone into bed that night he would wonder whether he would ever be clean again.

A JAMAICAN HALLOWEEN STORY

Even though they weren't working like they used to, Errol sat on the side of his bed, took the capsules in his palm and swallowed them. The signs were already there: weight loss, vomiting, losing his hair, and now the "visions". Dr. Lawrence, who had bandaged, stitched and healed his every wound, had checked Errol's eyes again. He shone the light into the brown eyes which from childhood had bulged from their sockets and made him look almost childlike and trusting. Those who were taken in by his boyish looks always paid dearly for their mistake.

"With your history of drug use, it's probably a complication from the natural progression of the disease – some brain damage and dementia."

This was the first time Errol thought that Dr. Lawrence didn't know what he was talking about. Errol had hallucinated when he'd smoked some weed laced with PCP, so he knew about hallucinations. These were different. These were visions.

"If it's any comfort, and I think that I can say this because you're a man who's seen death and is not afraid of it. In about three months it will all be over. No more visions."

Errol had felt like killing him right there, but he didn't. Dr. Lawrence was right. Errol had seen a lot of death and it didn't scare him. Besides killing Dr. Lawrence would only have made matters worse.

Errol reached for a glass of water on the nightstand and glanced over at the full-length mirror beside the bathroom. For six months he'd been asking Marcia, the girl who helped him, to take it down, but she never had. She was always busy sponging everything with bleach. He had to admit she did a good job at keeping the house clean, so he didn't complain.

But now he had to look at himself, a living duppy, mawga down to the bone. Errol had tried everything to keep the weight on – smoking weed and then eating as much food as he could, but it would only end up in the toilet. And the weed made the visions worse. He wanted to throw the glass into the mirror, but he needed his strength. His luck was bad enough as it was.

Errol sipped the water and looked through the window. Marcia was leaving in a hurry.

"Marcia, where you going? Rita not here yet!"

Marcia turned, looked back at him, and ran through the gate. By the look on her face, he knew she wasn't coming back. To hell with her.

Back in the good days, he'd had ten Marcias and prettier too. Much prettier. But it was the Marcias who'd given him this. Back then, no Marcia would have dared to leave him or she would have been a dead Marcia. Now, not even ugly Marcias respected him.

Still, he couldn't understand the look on her face. She was rushing as if she was late for church. He pulled out the drawer on his nightstand. The money was gone. The only thing that Marcia had left was his gun, which she never touched.

"You make too much duppies with that thing."

"Which thing, this?" He pointed to the gun, "Or this?" He unzipped his fly.

"The two of them." She walked to the door. "Mr. Thompson, why you do these things? You know I'm a Christian girl."

"I do it because I like to."

Now the Christian had robbed him and he didn't have the strength to teach her a lesson. But that was a Christian for you. If it wasn't the preacher tithing you into poverty, like they did to his mother before she became a Warner woman and gave up all her money to save him, then it was the priest robbing the little boys of their innocence in the confession box. It was a good thing he never believed in those things.

If he'd had even half his strength he would have chased her and given her a beating, but the thought of running after her made him feel weak.

He had to stay awake.

Reaching inside the drawer, Errol searched around and pulled out the bottle of NoDoze. At least she had left him the pills. They would keep him awake until Rita came.

The clock beside the bed rang and he turned it off. It was already six o'clock. Rita should have been there already. Had she left him too?

Errol wanted to get up, but he couldn't. He thought that if he left the room and went out to the gate, he could stay awake through the night. Not that the visions didn't come during the day, but if the angel of death came and told him he had a choice between dying during the day or at night, he would have chosen the day. Dying at night, surrounded by darkness, was too dread. But it wasn't the Angel of Death that he feared. He could handle her when she came and he hoped she would come quickly.

Errol looked over at the clock again. A minute past six. Rita was always there at six. Sometimes at five-thirty.

He would find a way to get out of bed. If he held on to the bedpost, he might have the strength to lift his body – he didn't weigh much now – and stagger to the bathroom. He placed his hand on the nightstand and reached for the bedpost.

It was no use. Now he was gasping for air. He had to control his breathing. He was always good at that. He had controlled his breathing and managed to stay still for two hours in a small closet until his boss was alone. That was how he'd made his boss a duppy, how he'd taken over.

But now his tired lungs were failing him. He didn't want to fall asleep. But now he could feel the tiredness race down his arms into his legs, and then back up to his thighs. He tried to fight it off, but it kept coming. It crept into his belly, up his chest, ignored his arms and crawled up his neck into his face and eyelids.

No, no, no, he screamed, like the battyboy whom he'd made a duppy. Errol remembered how the battyboy had begged and said that he had a wife and family. Errol loved it when they begged.

"You leave pum-pum for batty? You deserve to dead."

Errol held the gun up to the battyboy's head. He loved shooting them in the head to see how the bone and brains splattered. It made him wonder how something so small and spongy that made everything work could end up on the floor, so that you could use a piece of stick and poke around in it like it was dog shit?

Then the battyboy started to cry and said he wanted to live. He died with the words on his lips.

Errol's eyelids were heavy and the darkness overcame him. He knew it wouldn't last long. He knew that when he opened his eyes, the visions would come and there would be no one to waken him – not Rita or Marcia. All the duppies he had made – and there were many, their eyes bulging with blood and pus – would be standing at the foot of his bed whispering and laughing with their keh-keh laugh, like it was coming from up them nose hole.

"We waiting for you, Errol. We waiting."

I WANT TO DISTURB MY NEIGHBOUR

I always hated Friday evenings. Friday evenings meant one thing: Bible Study. Now don't get me wrong, I'm not a heathen. Never was, never claimed to be. It's just that every – and I mean *every* – Friday evening, when all my friends were out partying, drinking, walking down Daisy Avenue with their boyfriends or girlfriends, having a good time, I had to stay home with my mother, my Aunt Shirley and at least one other church brother or sister while they prayed and studied the Bible way into the night, to be saved from the judgment at hand.

Now if I had an easy life, like some of my friends, it wouldn't be so bad. Let's say if Bible study came after an afternoon of kicking back with a copy of *Mad* magazine or reasoning with a group of idren talking about the establishment of a u – no, *Itiopia* in which weed would be legal, you could hear reggae on the radio all hours of the day, pork would be illegal, and a man could somehow, without real effort or excitement, find himself blessed with several queens who would all get along – you know, African stylee.

But, no, Bible study came after I'd washed the dishes, cleaned my room and cooked dinner. And it always followed the same routine. Aunt Shirley or my mother would call me out of my room to meet their guest. I would take my time to come out, wave and mumble a polite hello, then shift my weight from leg to leg as my aunt and mother explained that I wasn't yet living in 'The Truth', which would make the guests – every single one of them – invite me to bow my head and pray with them. I would refuse and they would come back with their second offer – to allow them to pray for me. The second they closed their eyes, I'd ease out of

95

the room and lay in bed and listen to bootleg tapes from Jah Love, my favourite sound system as I twirled my Afro into something dread and hand-wrote music reviews for *Yout' Talk*, my school newspaper, while they prayed for my soul through the night.

So, on "the day in question", as Sammo, our local Babylon would call it, I was in my room – ours was one of these prefabricated Jamaican houses: louvre windows, gauzy yellow curtains, tile floors, dark wood bed with an iron spring and a trunk full o' old clothes, walls covered with posters of soul singers and Third World revolutionaries and a dresser with doilies and bottles of Big Wheel, Brut and Old Spice colognes – when the herald of Dean Fraser's horn (like the angel that broke the seventh seal) slid through the window. I knew I was in trouble.

"Courtneigh!"

I didn't answer. What would have been the point? I knew why my mother was calling me. She wanted to run off her mouth 'pon me about the music, as if it wasn't coming from somebody else's house.

I knew exactly where it was coming from. She knew where it was coming from. The house behind us, which was owned by a Rasta idren named Jah Mick. We'd grown up with Jah Mick. He used to be my older brother's closest friend and they'd both gotten soccer scholarships to the States. Jah Mick had gone up as Michael, what society people like my mother used to call "a decent boy". But he'd come back six months ago with a new name and a new flex, a beard and long dreads – a "boogooyagga". You don't need no translation. So it mean, so it sound. Say it, "Boo-goo-yagga. Boo-goo-yagga." It sound bad, eh?

Now I knew why Jah Mick had turned up the music like that. He'd started up a magazine named *Rootsman Kulcha* – a magazine that my mother was sure the prime minister was going to ban any day now. She was probably right.

Whenever Jah Mick was short of inspiration, he'd turn up the heat on his old tube amp and the air would be thick with the rumble of sweet dubwise. In the meantime, my mother's temper began its slow burn.

"Courtneigh Clifford Robinson! Come here right now!"

I went into the living room expecting to see a parade of the usual suspects on the big green sofa. But there in all his splendour was my Uncle Tyrone. Uncle Tyrone was saved? Uncle Tyrone (whose last name should have been Appleton) praying over my lost soul? When did this happen? My second thought was: does Aunt Shirley know about the go-go at the *Stable* who produced a little filly on the side? I held in my laughter when I saw him and he avoided my eyes.

"Courts," my mother said as she flattened the pleats on her stiff blue dress with the same severity with which she always starched and ironed on Thursday nights, "I want you to do me a favour. Be a good boy and promise me that you will do whatever I ask. You promise?"

She turned to Uncle Tyrone.

"Tell me first what I'm promising."

"What? You don't trust your own mother?" asked Uncle Tyrone.

"No, that's not what I'm saying."

"Then promise without questioning."

"Okay, I promise."

"Okay, now remember you promised. I want you to go over to your friend's house," – she gritted her teeth when she said *friend* – "and tell him to turn down that godforsaken music."

"How do you know is over there it coming from?"

"Who else plays that kind of music 'round here?"

"I don't know…"

"Look. Don't form fool with me. I have ears. I can hear. Is Michael alone who plays that kinda boogooyagga music. Is spite him trying spite me. Why him playing it so loud on a Friday night?"

"Ma…"

She turned to Uncle Tyrone. "Is Satan you know. Is Satan."

"Ma, you can listen to me for a minute. Not that I trying to cause any problems or anything but –"

"Who you shouting at?"

"Ah not shouting, Ma. But I have to talk up because you say the music loud."

"So the music don't sound loud to you?"

"That's beside the point –"

"Don't pass your place with me, y'hear."

Uncle Tyrone, his voice quivering, joined in. "Boy reach fourth form and ready to turn man!"

"So why you blaming me, Ma?"

"I just can't take it. This is the kinda thing that cause a place to get run down. Next thing you start to see people from Standpipe start to come 'round here because they think somebody keeping dance. And when that start to happen, every piece o' clothes disappear off the line."

"So Ma, if the music is such a botheration, why you don't tell him when you see him? You know him from him small. Him not going bite you."

"No. I can't talk to all him again. Him gone to the dogs. Head boy at St. George's College. Gone to the dogs."

"That's how he is when he's working on a project."

I turned to go back to my room.

"The only project he's working on is blaspheming! Talking 'bout Haile Selassie is God! He is a blasphemer! From now on I'm going to ban you from associating with blasphemers! Don't you ever set foot over there. If you ever set foot over there you cannot come back in this house. Boogooyagga music come mash up my Bible study like how ganja mash up that boy's mind. Stop."

She held her arms out to the side and cocked her head. "You hear that? Boom-chicki-boom. Boom-chicki-boom. You think I can take this whole night? And he used to be such a nice, good boy. His mother used to sing at Kingston Parish Church. She was an alto in the choir until…"

I could have said the words for her, "the divorce". Jah Mick's father had divorced his mother just as Jah Mick was about to go to the States. This, according to my mother, was the reason for the change – a blast from the past – a broken home.

My mother was finally thinking about divorcing my father, though she was afraid that something dreadful would happen to me, so she spent a lot of time praying for me, when she should have been praying for my father to come home.

My father was an accountant, a good one at that. And because of this he was often called away to audit hotels and sugar estates. Short trips would last three days, but it wasn't strange for him to be away for weeks. In that time he'd rarely call. But women would from time to time. My mother took her own accounting. Whoops! Another outside child.

"Ma, I have a headache. And my stomach not feeling so well. I can go and lie down?"

"After you go over to the house and tell him to turn down the music."

"I thought I wasn't supposed to go over there. You confusing me now."

"Hurry up and go and come back. I will make some Andrews."

"I don't have a headache, Ma. Nothing not bothering me."

"So is lie you was telling?"

Now she was testing me. She knew better than that.

"No, Ma. I just can't take this any more. Everything ah say is a fight. Everything him do is a fight. The man just playing some music. Is not a crime."

She glanced at Aunt Shirley and Uncle Tyrone, then crossed her arms. Looking at me squarely she said, "If you don't go over there and tell him to turn it down, I going to call Superintendent Samuels and tell him that he has ganja in the house."

"Ma!"

"Ma what?"

"You'd really do that?'

"No, but that is not the point." She glanced at Aunt Shirley and Uncle Tyrone again. "God forgive me. Tell him that I am very distressed about the music and that I cannot have my Bible study, and that I'm going to call the police because I suspect he has ganja over there if he doesn't do it."

"But you said you wouldn't do it, Ma. So what's the point?"

"I don't care who is involved, you have to listen to me."

"I thought I wasn't suppose to tell no lie."

"Nobody not asking you to tell a lie. I'm asking you to tell a lie? I'm giving you a message to give somebody. Who's to tell if I might change my mind? I might call Superintendent Samuels. Yes, if him go on like him bad and have hard ears, Sammo wi' know what to do with him. This is a residential area, after all. Nice, cool Friday evening and all you can hear is boom-chicki-boom. The place gone to the dogs, man. Gone to the dogs."

When my mother got like that, there was no arguing. I would have to do what she said.

I looked deep into Aunt Shirley's eyes because I didn't want to go over to Jah Mick's, but she turned away. I thought I could depend on her. She was always the fair one, even if she was a fanatic.

"Your mother is right," she said when she couldn't take my staring any more. "We can't study the Bible with all this noise. I don't know why that boogo-yagga bwai can't respect decent people and turn down that ole nayga music. I can barely hear myself think with all this boom..."

"Chicki boom," said Uncle Tyrone. From the way he held his head, I could tell it was more than the Holy Spirit that was running through his body.

"Uncle T..."

"You hair need a trim."

"Go now and I want you back here. I have something special that I want you to do for me."

"What you want me to do, Ma?"

"When you come back, you will see."

"At least give me a hint."

"It's a special visitor from our church. He won't be here again for a long time."

"Who is it?"

"Can't tell you. Hurry and come back."

I walked out of the living room and into the kitchen. The curried chicken and the rice were done. I turned off the heat under them.

"Courtneigh!"

"Yes, Ma."

"Come here before you leave."

I walked back into the living room.

"Remember your promise. Tell that man everything like I said it to you."

"Everything?"

"Just like I said. Word for word."

"Word for word."

"You promise me."

Her eyes burned into me.

"Yes, Ma."

I could have walked through the gate, but I jumped over the fence. Talk about flirting with danger. The fence was lined with a prickly bush. But it wasn't just this. My mother called anyone who jumped the fence a boogooyagga. That's how ole nayga come to grab clothes off the line you know. Over the fence. If my mother had seen me jumping over the fence, she would have hailed me with a million and one questions: Had I ever seen my father jump a fence? No. Any member of his family? No. Any member of hers? No. Well, yes, but I couldn't tell her that.

Uncle Tyrone used to jump fence when he had a woman up by Arailia Avenue. Those was the days before the Fosbury Flop. Uncle Tyrone was in the bedroom doing him business when him hear her husband car pull up in the carport. Uncle T took a Western roll over the top of a big rose bush and a prickle hook him in him pants' crotch. In the rush him did forget to put on him underpants and when the pants tear, two guinep and a Chiney banana drop out and a next door neighbour helper bawl, "And him love talk 'bout plantain."

How was I going to tell Jah Mick he had to turn down his music or my mother was going to call the Babylon? I wasn't going to lie to Ma the way my father had.

It was about the threat as much as the lie. The man wasn't doing anything really, yet she thought it was okay to terrorize him with the name of the police like she was casting out a demon: "In the name of Jesus come out!!!!!!!!!"

We accept the Rastaman today. We see him and his fashion victims all around – the colours, the music, the hair, the food. But in those days in Jamaica decent people like my mother thought they were surely the "generation of vipers" that signalled the coming of the last days. The acts of their ungodliness were everywhere. Decent girls were being seduced. Decent boys were dreading up their good, good hair and swearing their allegiance to Selassie. Rasta was as seductive as sin and the music was sperm and blood. They had to be stopped before their gospel spread to the young or all would be lost. It would have to come from the police.

Of course, Sammo, our police chief had the solution. He proposed it at our community center: "Trim them hair. Crack them skull. Beat them down." His words came to me as I walked along the uneven pavement and listened to the music coming from Jah Mick's house. As I kept repeating them, they created a space between the drum and the bass, and their riddim was transformed into a kind of chant.

Trim them hair.
Crack them skull.
Beat them down
Boof
Beat them down …
Keep them down
This is how de policeman
Deal with the Rasta
Boof, boof.
Trim them hair.
Comb them beard.
Crack them skull.
Kick them down.
This is how the policeman
Deal with rude bwais
Boof, boof, boof

"Natty Dread" streamed through the mango trees thick with yellow and red blossoms as I walked down Plumbago Path, then up Gardenia and around to Geranium to meet Jah Mick – the man who had taught me to do the layout for our school yearbook.

"If you can't separate wheat from chaff, you will end up mawga and poor," he teased. Sometimes he seemed to know me better than myself. When I told him how home was, he said he knew the tribulations I was going through, for he had gone through them too, until he had decided to become a dreadlock – and then the tribulations weren't gone, they just changed.

Jah Mick was my bridge to the Jamaica that was changing in front of my eyes, my mother's eyes, my aunt's eyes. Everyone but Uncle Tyrone's, whose eyes were closed most of the time.

I would never be a true Rasta. I would hang on to my pride and my doubts about all religions. In the midst of the smoke, the weed, the reasoning with the brethren, I held firm and the brethren it seemed respected me. I would not budge.

I looked up to the hills. My mother was right; this was not a paradise. Up in the hills, the Nyahbinghi were smoking weed and chanting down Babylon. Down the road in Standpipe, they were lighting up a chalice and climbing toward Mount Zion.

I walked firmly up the middle of Geranium where Jah Mick lived. The pathway to his verandah was lined with bougainvilleas that looped around the house to the grilled carport.

I didn't know which was beating louder: the music or my heart.

When I got to the gate of the man who was teaching me everything about the Jamaica being wished for and worked at by my classmates and friends, I turned around and took some fast steps back down the block. Houses that I'd passed in a trance only minutes before became concrete to me. You know what I mean – not concrete like concrete – but real, alive – alive with real meaning. Junior's house. David's house. Dennis's house, Gail's house, Jennifer's house. Maxine's. All friends from short pants and marble days till now. None of them were home. They were in the park, either playing football or watching the game before they went to the movies when the sun went down.

I was in a panic now. What if my mother was right? What if all my friends and I were going to die because we didn't believe in her God. All of my friends. And their friends and their friend's friends. People I didn't even know. All of them condemned… unless of course they changed. All our lives and loves would disappear in fire and ash because we didn't believe.

Many of my friends were Rasta, smoking weed, having a good time. They weren't evil, maybe just lost. I could understand my mother's concern. She said all I had to do was repent of my ways and I would be saved. All I had to do was play my cards right and she, Aunt Shirley, Uncle Tyrone (now that he was on the road to redemption) and I would all be saved, stuck together, forever on a paradise earth. But who'd want to be with Uncle Tyrone for all eternity?

I pushed through the gate and could see Jah Mick in the living room.

"I would never be Rasta," I told myself. "Never. Never. Never." I pumped my arms harder. "Never. Never. Never."

At this point I heard his voice: "You warming up?"

Jah Mick had been watching me. I could tell he was feeling irie because he'd taken off his black tracksuit and was sitting cross-legged in front of a speaker, a towel draped loosely around his neck. When I stepped inside off the verandah he tucked his dreads into his tricolour tam and smiled from deep inside the bush of his moustache and beard. The green carpet felt fat beneath my feet. The room was as it was when his parents lived there – heavy brown drapes that never opened, Morris chairs, a mahogany breakfront with shelves and shelves of figurines and framed paintings of sunsets and tropical birds on the walls.

"So little lion," said Jah Mick. "What you defending today?"

I didn't answer. My tongue was in my throat. Eventually I said, "Nothing."

He laughed. "You can't defend nothing, little lion. You mus' always defend somep'n. If you don't stand for something you wi' fall fo' anything."

"So how the magazine coming?" I asked, trying to get away from the reasoning.

He shook his head. "Not so good. That's why you see me here trying to hold a vibes. The music kinda loud. Come talk to me in the room."

The room was where he slept and worked. It had a velvet poster of Haile Selassie on the door and lots of soccer posters on the walls – Pele, Beckenbauer, Eusebio and Cruyff – and furniture that looked like mine.

Through the wall the music had dulled to a blobby throb, but the layout on the drafting table buzzed. He kept his books in the other bedrooms. Books that I'd borrowed and read in secret… Garvey, Kenyatta, Fanon…

"I want to talk to you," I mumbled.

"You cool?"

"No… no. That's why ah need to talk to you."

I couldn't say it. I started and stopped many times, until he said sternly, "Talk up, man. Talk up. You mother never teach you to talk up?"

"My mother," I began. "My mother…"

"Yes."

"My mother…"

"Yes. Say it."

"My mother say you mus' …"

"Mus'?"

He stood now and went over to the drafting table. He stood in a way that put his back to me.

Jah Mick never took kindly to anyone telling him anything that he had or didn't have to do.

"My mother says you must turn down the music."

He took a deep breath, and then breathed out calmly.

"And if I don't?"

"She goin'…"

"Goin' wha'?"

"Well, she say…"

"Say wha'?"

"She say she goin' call Sammo and tell him you have ganja over here."

He turned to face me now and I turned my back to him.

"I have ganja over here?" he blurted. He sounded like a young head boy who'd been accused of cheating on a test. "I have ganja over here? Your mother say she goin' tell Sammo I have ganja over here?" His voice deepened into anger now. "So wha'? You support that?"

I turned around to face him.

"Wha' you think?"

He stepped right up to me and put his hand on my shoulder, which made me jerk and wince. I woulda understand if him did lick me.

"No ganja not here. I don't smoke and I don't allow nobody to' smoke over here. And you know that. So how you coulda come to me with a message like that?"

"Don't act like you don't know how she stay," I said with irritation. "You make it seem like is my fault that you turn dread and she turn to the Lord. The two o' oonoo come in like crosses.

Just turn down the music, nuh. Just make life easy, nuh. She is a old lady. She can't change. Certain kinda music goin' burn her. And when it burn her is me she take it out 'pon. Is not you. You is a big man. You live by yourself. Me still live with my mother and she taking your fat and frying me."

"So wha'? Is my fault that your mother is a pagan heart? Miss B used to be a nice lady, then she make this church thing fly inna her head and now is like ah living in a prison. Every Friday evening is this singing and praying. Eleven o'clock o' night and them still going on. Is wha' so, El Paso? Them don't have any consideration? Them only business 'bout themselves?"

Before I could answer he pressed on. "And is not me alone complaining bout it. Is nuff people in the area start to complain that people knocking on their gate, and when they go out there is somebody want to give them a pamphlet or invite them to a meeting. Bredrin, none o' this was going on before your mother found the Lord, so everybody know is because o' she. Most people round here grow up Anglican and Catholic. They don't too like this Jehovah Witness thing."

He dropped his voice into a whisper now. "Not that I'm passing judgment... but... you know, people have it as a cult."

"Jah Mick, she is still my mother, you know."

He wiped his forehead with the towel and looked up at the ceiling

"So what you want me to do?" I asked and walked around him. I puttered around looking at the drafting table, as if the conversation was done. The layout was in trouble. If he needed music to inspire him he needed to turn it up some more.

"You know if the police come here, they going to bring ganja to find..."

"Yes."

"So what you going do?"

"I already do it. I tell you what she asked me to tell you and now is up to you."

"Yes, you do that, but you more than do that. You done it too."

He took a deep breath, and then blew it slowly through his mouth. Our friendship was over and he wanted me to think that it was all my fault.

"Turn off the set when you leaving."

He sat down on the bed again.

"You not fair, Jah Mick. You not fair."

"Just turn it off," he said slowly. "Just turn it off. I have to go back to work. I need peace and quiet for that."

"So is my time to leave?"

"Not saying that. Just saying is my time to work."

Before I closed the door to his bedroom I said, "So you have me up now, Jah Mick."

"Shame o' you, man. Shame o' you. Jah love everybody. You know that already. Tonight before I and I go to sleep I and I goin' pray for you … ask Jah to protect you in the midst of the heathen. Fret not thyself, little lion. When revolution come all pagan heart goin' get what is theirs."

He smiled now and pointed to the hair beneath his tam. "But by dem time deh you wi' truly know yourself and grow your covenant. So when the judgment come, Jah Jah wi' watch over the I. You let me down, but I and I overstand. You living under pagan influence daily so some o' it must rub off. Stand firm till such time though. Stand firm. Vengeance is mine. So Jah say. Vengeance is mine."

I could have said a lot of things before I left. But what would have been the point?

I opened the door to the living room. I thought about my mother and her hallelujahs, Aunt Shirley and Uncle Tyrone and the guests who would be coming by that night. I had kept my promises, and I hadn't lied.

After that I didn't pray for a very long time.

BOBBY BIJANI AND THE ROLLING CALF

"There, you hear it?"

Bobby nudged his wife, Audrey, who was fast asleep beside him. He tapped her on her shoulder.

"What you want, Bobby?" Audrey glanced at the clock. "Is three o'clock in the morning."

"You don't hear it?"

"Hear what, Bobby?"

Bobby hesitated. He knew he sounded foolish, but it wasn't the first time that he'd heard the sound, and every time he heard it, nothing good ever happened after that.

He'd been hearing the rattling of the chains ever since he'd inherited his uncle's house in Westmoreland. At first, Bobby thought it was his uncle's duppy come to visit him. He'd hoped that it was something else, like a car breaking down or tow truck, but it sounded too much like the time he first heard a rolling calf when his uncle was almost beaten to death by some gunmen in Westmoreland. He had saved his uncle's life by hiding him in a cistern.

Bobby heard the chains rattling again.

"Audrey, you going tell me you don't hear it this time?"

"What I supposed to hear, Bobby?"

"You promise you won't laugh?"

"Laugh? I trying to get some sleep. Just tell me and let me go back to sleep."

"You promise you won't laugh. Promise me."

"I promise."

"You sure?"

"Yes."

108

"Rolling calf."

Audrey laughed and double wrapped the comforter around her waist as tightly as she covered herself every night when she finally came to bed.

"You promised me you wouldn't laugh."

She looked at him over her shoulder.

"Rolling calf?"

"Yes."

"In Miami?"

"Yes."

"Bobby, you must be going mad. Get some sleep."

Audrey glanced at the clock again and put the pillow over her head. She was determined nothing else was going to rouse her from her hard-earned sleep.

But Bobby couldn't sleep and he knew he wasn't going mad. Maybe it was the wind. But he was afraid of looking through the window, for if the rolling calf's eyes met his, it would have torn him apart, and he still hadn't found his penknife. So he stayed up in the bed for three hours listening to the rolling calf going round and round the block until the rooster that belonged to Mr. Gonzalez, who had just moved from Hialeah, frightened it away.

When Bobby was sure the rolling calf was gone, he went outside to get the newspaper and then made coffee for Audrey, who would soon be leaving for work at HRS. As he was making the coffee, he checked the mail and noticed another offer from a private company offering Audrey a job with a raise and even more benefits than the government. Audrey had probably turned down that job as well. He often wondered why Audrey would turn down these positions – which were the same kinds of work, but for people who could pay, not like the hard-luck cases at HRS. But that was Audrey. Always a soft spot for losers.

That's why she was always tired and slept so soundly. The sleep of the innocent. He envied her for that. She could sleep through a hurricane. In fact, she had. When Hurricane Wilma swept through Miami, she turned on the television and when she found out that she didn't have to go to work, she turned off the television and slept for the next thirty-six hours.

Audrey hadn't woken then until his brother, Alex, (his half-brother really) showed up at the house looking for food and water. Alex hadn't saved a thing and wasn't prepared for the hurricane, so she gave him something to eat. All of the money that Alex earned as a waiter at Carlton's Restaurant went into entertaining one woman after another, just to get a little sex.

Bobby was sure Alex was a sex addict. It wasn't that *he* didn't like sex. It was good. But it wasn't like how Alex would go on about it. And then, after every romance was over, he would show up at Bobby's house, penniless and heartbroken.

Bobby couldn't understand him. A man could never control a woman, but he could at least control his money. Alex couldn't control either, and after the women broke his heart, he would come over to Bobby's house to drink a couple of Red Stripes and spend hours poring over their photo albums, especially the pictures of Bobby's wedding day when their parents were still alive, and pining over all the opportunities he had missed to settle down and have some kids.

Bobby had never wanted kids. As he told Audrey, they only spent your money and never paid you back. Indeed, one morning without telling her, he went out and had a vasectomy. He was sore for a week. She didn't talk to him for a month.

During that time, Alex seemed to be over at their home more than usual, studying the photo albums, and sighing about how pleased he'd been to bring a little happiness in women's lives. By that he meant sex.

Sometimes Bobby wondered if *he* had been the illegitimate child because Alex was more like his father than he was. Edwin, their father, used to supply the novelty shops in MoBay with goods he bought in Miami. On one trip down to MoBay, Alex was conceived. Bobby didn't know of Alex until the funeral when he called him from Jamaica and told him about their father's death. Alex had apologized that he could not help to pay for the funeral. Bobby had paid for everything.

Alex showed up at the funeral in what looked like a borrowed suit and dirty shoes. But he was the dead stamp of their father in more ways than one. From the first time Bobby met him, he knew he had met a younger version of his father: a smooth-talking Jamaican man who could talk a crab out of her shell.

Bobby finished making the coffee and opened the sports section to check out how the Miami Heat had been playing. He was also trying to figure out a way to talk with Andrew, the security guard at the supermarket where he worked. Andrew's father had been an obeah man in Jamaica and women were always going to him to get explanations of their dreams.

"How you and the rolling calf this morning?" Audrey asked.

"I know I shouldn't have told you anything."

Audrey had already packed her briefcase and was dressed in a new cream pants-suit. She had barely noticed how Bobby's clothes had begun to hang off him. How he now resembled a stick in pajamas.

"I'm just teasing you, Bobby. Take it easy."

"No, this is a serious thing. It keeping me up at night."

"Bobby, rolling calf should be the least of your problems. More serious things happening around you."

"Like what?"

"You need help, Bobby."

Bobby wondered what she meant, but by the time he thought of asking her, she was already through the door with her coffee mug in her hand. Not even a kiss any more. Not even breakfast together any more. He cursed himself for not responding more quickly, but he had a lot of things on his mind.

It shouldn't have been a big thing, but the rolling calf was keeping him up late at night and he was falling asleep on the job. His boss, Frantz la Fontaine, had found him asleep on a stack of large Purina Cat Chow bags and told him he'd fire him if he found him sleeping on the job again.

Bobby appealed to Josh Hardy, the new manager, but he told him that Mr. Fontaine was his boss and he had to do what his boss told him. So whatever was bothering him, he needed to get it out of the way and get back to his life.

Bobby understood Josh's position. Josh was still a boy to him and everyone knew that he had only gotten the position after he had pushed out Alvaro, the former assistant manager and begun sleeping with his wife. Not that the Cuban guy knew. That was a secret amongst the Jamaican men. Up to the week before the rolling calf appeared, Bobby had been helping Alvaro lift the bags of cat chow, so that he could leave early and Josh could go and have sex with Alvaro's wife.

But Bobby didn't want to jeopardize his situation with Josh. He didn't want Josh to fire him before the final papers from the probate court in Jamaica came through, and he would be named as the sole inheritor of his uncle's estate in Jamaica. Then Bobby could sell his house in Miami and retire to Westmoreland.

Before he left for work, Bobby checked the mail again. He wondered what was causing the delay. Had the courts found out that he had a brother? Was Alex was entitled to a share of the estate? He had double-checked everything. Legally, Alex had never existed. He didn't have a birth certificate and everything else about him was illegal. And why should Alex get any money? He was an "outside" child. He'd never had to put up with their father's rages, his stinginess, and his uncle's shame with those little boys. Why, after all he had been through, should he share the inheritance with Alex? Besides, Alex didn't know about the case and what he didn't know wouldn't hurt him.

There wasn't any mail from Jamaica. Bobby locked the door and drove down to the supermarket. Standing outside the service entrance, he saw Andrew sitting on top of the crates, wearing his felt hat, dark glasses, and dark blue uniform. He was smoking Matterhorn, the only brand of cigarettes he'd ever smoked.

When Andrew moved to Miami, he'd scoured all the stores until he found a small store on 163rd Street that sold Matterhorns. And even though every morning he started his day with coughs that echoed through the house, when his wife begged him to quit, he told her that Matterhorns wouldn't give anyone cancer because they were menthol and so were medicine. And if anyone knew about medicine – not Babylon medicine, but the true-true medicine from Africa – then it was him.

Bobby got out of his car and decided against the small talk about sports. He pulled a pack of Matterhorn out of the glove compartment and held it tightly in his hand. Bobby was going to be direct because things were getting out of hand.

The minute Andrew saw Bobby, he shouted out, "Man, you look like you need some Nutrament, some stout and egg, or some Irish moss! What make you look so mash up?"

Bobby knew he was with a real obeah man the minute Andrew said that. A true obeah man knew not only the science of herbs, but also knew the people around them, so that when trouble began, he could help them find a way out.

"If you know that, then you must know everything."

Andrew jumped down off the crates and moved closer to him.

"Any fool could see how you mawga down. How much pounds you lose."

"Twenty, maybe thirty."

"And you never have much to start with. You sure you healthy? You have a woman on the side that you pick up something?"

"I have one woman in my life. Why would I want more?"

"Your business that. So how I can help you? What bothering you? That's the only reason people come to me – when something bothering them."

Bobby handed Andrew the pack of Matterhorn and he put them in his pocket.

"I know *you* won't laugh."

"Why should I laugh at a man's worries?"

Bobby hesitated.

"My wife laughed at me when I told her about my worries."

"That is something you have to work out with her. Me never come between man and wife. God say so. So if is that, me can't help you."

"Josh and Mr. Fontaine say if they catch me sleeping in the warehouse again them going fire me."

"That is you and them business. Me is just a security guard. But that is not what bothering you."

"How you know?'

"You have the glow around you of a man that crosses following."

"How you know."

"Deep science. So tell me what really bothering you?"

Bobby stuck his hands in his pockets and looked down at the floor. He might as well say it. It would not have been the first time that Andrew heard something like this.

"Rolling calf."

Andrew put out his cigarette and flicked the butt onto the

driveway. He pulled out the new pack of Matterhorns and lit another one. He blew the smoke into the air and all over Bobby.

"You sure?"

Bobby coughed.

"Sure."

"How long it been bothering you?"

"Three months now. I can't sleep at night."

"Man, drink two whites and go to sleep."

"I tried that and it didn't work. I even tried some sleeping pills. They never work either."

"First: wrong move. Babylon medicine only make to make them richer. That's why them not curing AIDS. More money to treat you than cure you. The only thing I can tell you is that when a rolling calf show up, there's a dark secret in your house that need to come out into the light. You have to confess."

Bobby wondered if Andrew knew about the inheritance.

"Confess what?"

"That is for you and the rolling calf. I only stand in between."

Bobby dug in his pocket and pulled out a twenty dollar bill. It pained him to give it, but it was customary. Andrew put the bill in the band of his felt hat, beside a rooster's tail-feather.

"I only want to know the answer to one question."

"What?"

"What a coolie man like you know about rolling calf?"

"Coolie-Royal! The royal side of me, from Africa know these things."

They knocked fists, and Bobby went off relieved that he knew how to get rid of the rolling calf. For the first time in ages, he didn't fall asleep at work. When he got home, he fell asleep until the rolling calf came rumbling down the street.

He went into the living room and, hiding behind the curtains, confessed all the little things he had done at work: stealing toilet paper and paper clips, calling in sick when he wasn't, but the rolling calf wouldn't go away. It continued roaring through the neighbourhood until Mr. Gonzalez's rooster frightened it away. Bobby confessed for three nights, but nothing worked and now every time Andrew saw him he only shook his head and walked away.

Bobby was making such a racket in the neighbourhood that

someone called the police who came by one evening and told him that if he didn't stop, they were going to issue him a citation.

He listened to the police carefully, but still continued every morning with his morning confessions. They irritated Audrey to the point that she had moved into the guest room. She wished they'd given him a citation because money was the only thing Bobby seemed to care about. If they'd given him a citation, then maybe she could get a good night's sleep without her husband sneaking out of their bed to go downstairs to scream out of the window and tell everybody their business.

If she wanted everyone to know her business, she would have gone back to church and sat beside Janice Simpson – "The Jamaican Internet" – who, the minute you told her anything, everybody in Miami, New York, London, Pembroke Pines, Lauderhill and Kingston knew, word for word. Now Bobby and his rolling calf were getting on her last nerve and she couldn't do anything.

The rolling calf wouldn't go away. Bobby kept on confessing until the police came back and issued the citation. This hit him where it hurt. This was money.

Finally, after another week of confessing and Andrew waking him up before Mr. Fontaine could find him sleeping, he blurted out to the rolling calf, "Yes, my brother don't know it, but I thiefing his inheritance."

The rolling calf stopped for a moment, sniffed the air and seemed to look over at the window. Bobby hid behind the curtains but the rolling calf kept galloping around the block dragging the chains behind it, sparks flying everywhere.

Bobby didn't know what to do. He went back to Andrew and told him everything.

"You sure you want to get rid of it? You sure you telling the truth? Everything you hiding?"

"Yes, man. It mashing up my life. I telling the truth – everything I was hiding."

"You sure is the rolling calf mashing up *your* life?"

"Yes... What you mean."

"I mean if it not harming you, then is best to leave things as they are. Be careful when you digging through things like this. Some things you don't want to find out."

"I willing to do anything now."

"All right. Is you say so."

Andrew gave Bobby a mirror and a penknife and told him to put them in front of his house. He said they would stop the rolling calf from moving, but it would make so much noise from the bawling that he'd better confess all that had to be known.

"It will stop. It can't go any further. It can only turn and go back where it came from."

For the first time in ages, Bobby worked the whole day and went home ready to try the mirror. He nailed it up in front of his house and dug the penknife into the ground where he usually put the garbage cans, and went to sleep.

At about three o'clock in the morning, the rolling calf came thundering down the street and stopped dead in its tracks at Bobby's house. It couldn't move and began making a terrible mournful sound that seemed to shake the windowpanes. Bobby thought about killing it with the machete he kept under his bed. But then he thought about its red eyes and how its horns could rip a man in two. And how do you kill a rolling calf?

He would confess and send it on its way. He confessed again that the papers had come, that he had now legally inherited his uncle's land, and that he was going to quit his job and move back to Jamaica and he didn't want the rolling calf to follow him around any more.

The rolling calf bellowed again and fire came out of its nostrils. The noise grew louder. Bobby was desperate. He began making up things he had never done like stealing from his mother, but it only made the rolling calf angrier. It looked like it was now ready to mash down the house.

Bobby began screaming.

"Is what you want? Is what you want? I tell you everything! Everything!"

The rolling calf dug its hooves into the asphalt and was getting ready to charge.

"Tell me what you want to know."

He was bending down by the window expecting the worst when Audrey brushed by him with her nightgown drawn tightly around her waist. She opened the window and screamed.

116

"Jesus Christ. What a woman have to do around here to get some sleep. I having sex with Alex, and it's so good that is the only reason I can sleep at night."

She slammed the window shut and went back to the guest room.

Bobby slowly got up from his knees and looked out of the window. The rolling calf was gone. He looked at his watch. It was only five o'clock.

He went back to sleep and when he woke up he called Josh and resigned from the supermarket. He packed his bags, closed up his bank accounts, and moved down to Jamaica to live in his big house that he had inherited from his uncle.

The last time he heard from Audrey, she sent a letter telling him that she and Alex were going to have a baby and that they wanted to get married. She said she'd forgiven him and that she wasn't contesting the will or anything to do with the inheritance in Jamaica. Bobby tore up the letter and burned it in the back yard under his favourite mango tree.

He never heard the rolling calf again.

FOUR SEASONS

In the room, dark except for the light of a smouldering fire, Alejandro sat in a mustard-coloured armchair, sipping scotch, and listening to the last bars of Vivaldi's "Four Seasons." From the first time he'd heard "Winter" on his tiny gramophone and dreamed of playing in a grand concert hall in Bogotá, he'd been struck by the similarity of *invierno* and *infierno*.

When he'd worked with the merchant marine, out in the blue Atlantic, and the refrain had swelled in his head, he'd known for certain they meant the same thing. Only the image of Ana with her long slender legs and boisterous laughter kept him from putting his gun to his mouth.

When Ana had given him his son, Alejo, he'd vowed his child would never have to bear the hardships of poverty. When he was eleven, his mother told him that his father (she always called him "El Doctor") had been killed by the communists and he was now the man of the house. "You'll have to take care of me and your brothers and sisters."

He'd cried when the eldest son from his father's "real" family took way the piano on which he used to play for his father. That was the day it seemed the whole of Cartagena watched as his family was forced out of the house and the neighbours made fun of him because he was now one of them, *un gamin*. The word stuck with him like a curse.

Alejandro took another sip of scotch, wiped his forehead with a handkerchief and dialled his son-in-law.

"Are you still coming? I have your Christmas present. Christmas is a time for coming together."

"It's okay, Alejandro," said Daniel. "I understand, I'll soon be over."

"I'm waiting."

Alejandro hung up. He would wait in the silence of the room. Like the lovers in the next apartment, he would allow the silence to wrap around him like a cocoon and wait in that black room that was so far away from Cartagena.

He closed his eyes and listened to the drip, drip, drip coming from the bathroom, like the sound of the faucet he'd never fixed when he and his family lived in Queens.

★

The sign had said, "Welcome to Marlboro Country," with the famous cowboy rounding up cattle. Alejandro had walked through the interminable corridors to find Ana waiting for him in Customs. She'd paid two thousand dollars to a lawyer in New York and he'd gotten his resident alien visa. They'd been married by proxy and now he was coming to the United States as her husband. That was not how he'd wanted it. He'd wanted a church wedding, a reception by the sea with Ana in a white dress, his brothers and sisters throwing white rice and congratulating him because he had protected and kept them alive all these years by selling coal, newspapers – anything to keep the family together.

Customs cleared his luggage and Ana stood by the door. She was crying. She looked as beautiful as the first day he saw her outside the Senate, waiting for a lover who was never coming back.

"*Mi amor.*" He clasped her in his arms and gently stroked her hair. Slowly he let her go, touched her stomach, and repeated his prayer to the Virgin Mary that his son's skin would be fair, like Ana's, and not clouded with his *mestizo* blood.

"How do you do?"

"You've been practising your English," she said. She hugged him and ran her fingers across his forehead,

"Ah, those lines. You get them from too much worrying. Don't worry. Ana will take care of you now. My Alejandro, my dear Alejandro."

He didn't understand what she'd said except that she'd said his name with such tenderness he felt like crying. But he couldn't. Not now.

"Alejandro, Alejandro, Alejandro!"

Two little girls dressed in white were running down the hallway. They'd been hiding behind the news racks.

They grabbed hold of his legs and held him as if they would never let go. Little Natalie, who sometimes seemed not to like men, was holding him the tightest. She loved playing with his hands, soft and smooth with the perfumed talc from the barbershop. Alejandro had learned to cut hair when he was at sea and had supported himself as a barber in Venezuela where he'd gone to school and earned a certificate.

Alejandro held Natalie in her arms and gave her some sweets he'd brought from Medellin. Her hair was long, almost down to her waist. Ana would have cut it, but she remembered what had happened the last time she'd tried.

"I am the barber in this house. I cut her hair." He had said this so fiercely Ana had been surprised by his passion. It could go in either direction. At times, tender. At other times, vicious.

"What about me?"

Alejandro laughed and gave Gloria some sweets as well.

"We are a family."

They had walked arm in arm towards the taxis, the girls trailing behind them, trying to get the wrappers off the candy. Ana signalled for a taxi and it pulled up to the other side of the street. The driver ran over and collected their luggage. They climbed into the car, then Ana had screamed, *Natalie! Donde esta Natalie?*

Natalie had been so preoccupied with the candy, she'd lost herself in the crowd.

Alejandro tried to open the door, but it had no handle. The door had to be opened from the outside.

The driver looked at Ana.

"What's the problem, ma'am?"

"My daughter, she is..." Ana tried to calm herself so the words would come out in English. She couldn't. She pointed frantically at Natalie. Alejandro was fumbling with the door.

"That's your daughter."

"*Si*. Yes."

"Okay, I'll go get her.'

The driver had run across the street to get Natalie, but she wouldn't move. He'd stretched out his hands, but she wouldn't go to him. The driver finally grabbed for her.

"Alejandro. Alejandro."

Natalie was running across the street into the oncoming traffic. There was a screech of brakes and a car stopped three feet away from her. Alejandro was furious. He had clambered past Ana and Gloria and run to pick up Natalie. She was hysterical. Alejandro held her in his arms and glared at the driver.

"*Negro imbecil.* I kill you if anything happen."

"What the fuck you say, spic?"

Ana had stood between the men. It was late and they needed the ride into Queens.

"What he call me?"

"It's nothing, nothing really."

"How much do I owe you, mister?"

"Nothing. I haven't taken you anywhere."

"We'll take another taxi then."

"That's all right. Just tell your man I was only trying to help."

The driver stalked past Alejandro, took the luggage out of the trunk, and put it on the sidewalk.

"I didn't want to go to your refried beans neighbourhood anyway."

The driver climbed into the front seat of the car.

"And hey, spic, learn to speak English. You're in America!"

The driver had been laughing as he drove off. It was the last thing that Alejandro saw as the taxi merged into the traffic. A black face with white teeth. Laughing at him.

*

Alejandro got out of the chair and walked over to the stereo. He knocked the picture of Natalie and her husband on their wedding day off the CD player they had given to him, a Christmas present he had never used.

The glass had been smashed, but they were still smiling as if nothing had happened. Natalie looked happy, but why? Hadn't she seen who she was marrying? Alejandro could never understand that.

He looked at the picture again. It had been a sunny day. The night before the wedding he and Ana had quarrelled. He was not going.

"But Alejandro, you've been more of a father to her than her real father."

He hadn't said anything.

"Why aren't you going? Why?"

"*No me gusta ir.*"

"I know the reason and it's stupid. And speak to me in English, you stubborn old man. You speak it well enough with your customers in your barbershop!"

Alejandro had hidden himself in his silence. It was a shield from which he refused to emerge. There would be no arguing. He had made up his mind.

"Well, she's my daughter. I'm going to her wedding. She's having the wedding we never had with the church and her brother and sister and the priest blessing the wedding. Not some public notary with rum on his breath and cigarette stains on his fingers. And Alejo is going. Daniel bought his suit and your son will be giving her away."

For a moment Alejandro left his den to look at the pictures Ana had collected over the years before she'd died from breast cancer. There were photos of Daniel and Natalie at his graduation, *magna cum laude*, from Howard University and the last picture of Gloria before she got a tattoo, left the house, and moved to South Beach. There was a charcoal drawing that Alejo had done of his mother.

His son had been determined to become an artist, but he had said no. There was no future. It would be a life of misery, pain, and poverty. That was why, even when they couldn't afford it, he'd sent Alejo to the best Catholic school in the city, while the girls went to public schools in Little Havana and then North Miami Beach.

Alejo had resented him for that and did everything he could

to be expelled until the principal gave in. The letter was sent to the barbershop just three months before Alejo was due to graduate. Alejandro begged and begged in his best broken English, but the principal, a Black man, just shook his head and said that Alejo had been giving too much trouble.

Natalie had told Daniel and he'd gone to the school and spoken to the principal. Ana had told him that Daniel had vouched personally for Alejo and said he'd make sure that he would change his behaviour. Daniel had persuaded the principal that Alejo wasn't a troublemaker, that he was just confused. If he gave Alejo extra time to work in the art room, he'd see a change in his behaviour.

The principal agreed and Alejo had been reinstated. Everything happened as Daniel had predicted. Alejo took his SAT and scored over 1500. The offers from colleges and universities began flooding the mailbox.

During the graduation ceremony, Alejandro had watched as Alejo mounted the steps and held his diploma in his hands. He waved to Natalie and Daniel and went off with them to dinner. They'd invited Alejandro, but he still refused to go out with Natalie and "*el negro*".

When Alejo came home the next day, Alejandro was happy. He'd opened the letter from Yale and was waving it in the air.

"*Hijomio. Buena noticia. Te han bacado a Yale.*"

"No, Papa. I've thought about it. I filled out those papers for you. I'm not going. I'm going to study art in California."

"California?"

"Yes. Daniel says…"

"*Todo es el maricon,* Daniel."

"No, I'm going to California."

"You do that, and you can leave this house."

"I don't care. Daniel will help me."

"*No mas con el hijo de puta*, Daniel. I'm your father. I will say what you do and don't. *No un negro como el.* He broke up our family with Natalie and that's why Gloria hates me. *No mas, hijo. No mas.*"

"Papa, I'm going to California. Daniel is outside, waiting in the car."

That was the last time he'd seen Alejo before he left for California, driving off in Daniel's car, both of them smiling. He had lost his son.

★

Alejandro went back to his den and poured himself another drink, the tears welling in his eyes. What kind of life did Alejo think he was going to have in California studying art? Was he gay and hiding it? Was Daniel helping him? Was Daniel having an affair with his son? He knew about men like that in Colombia and on the ship. He had almost finished the bottle of whisky.

"*Yo soy el padre. Yo dijo que es y no que es...*"

The tears trickled down his face as he walked over to his briefcase where he kept his scissors and the revolver that had been his companion on so many nights when he was alone and locking up the barbershop all by himself. The last time he used the gun was when two black *gamines* had tried to hold him up, but he'd shown them he wasn't a scared *viejo*. He'd shot one of them, but he lived. The other had run away.

There were footsteps in the doorway and the door bell rang. It was Daniel. Alejandro slipped the bullets into place. He checked the revolver. There were two bullets in the chamber. He wasn't going to miss.

"*Yo soy el padre. Hijo de puta.*"

In the grate, the dying embers from the burnt dry branches made popping sounds, and sparks flickered upwards through the chimney into the night. The face of the moon was covered by clouds. He dropped the needle back on the record, on the groove for "Winter". The room was filled again with the sound Vivaldi's music. It would block any other sounds that would disturb the neighbours.

THE DAY JESUS CHRIST CAME TO MOUNT AIRY

"Jesus Christ, Macky!"

"Woman, don't take my name in vain."

My mother shut her mouth the minute we heard the voice outside the front door. With her fingers over her lips she motioned to me to do the same.

But whoever it was wasn't going away.

"Is who that?"

"It's me, Jesus."

I could see the fear in my mother's eyes. She pointed to the back door and I knew what to do.

"I soon come, Mister. I have to put on some clothes."

While my mother was putting on one of my father's jackets – he wouldn't be needing them any more because he was in jail in Florida – I slipped through the trap door in the kitchen to see who it really was.

From underneath the house, I saw a brown man with curly hair wearing a Bob Marley T-shirt, blue jeans and Jesus boots. He looked harmless because he didn't have a gun or knife in his pants leg or in the back or side of his waist. I scoped him out for about five minutes, and then ran back to tell my mother.

"How you feel about him, Macky?"

"He looks soft."

My mother went over to the window and *pripsed* the fellow by the door. She took a long, hard look at him and came back to the door.

"What you want, Mister?"

"Nothing. I'm just tired and I come to spend the night with you."

"No, sir. No. No. No. You can't come spend the night with me. I don't know what those girls been telling you down by the hotel, but I'm a respectable married woman. You better leave right now because my son gone to wake up my husband and if he catch you outside, the door, well…"

"You're right that your husband sleeping, but he's sleeping in jail."

My mother gasped and pulled the jacket over her chest.

"But he's coming home soon, Darlene. He's coming home. All the prayers that you've been saying by your bedside, as you walk down the hill, and while you're eating dinner with Macky, are going come true because he loves you."

Before I could say, "Wait, mama," she opened the door and looked at the man.

"How you know all that? I hope you is not one of Gerald's bad man friend. If you are a gunman, I can tell you we don't have no money. The government take away everything. All we have is this little house."

"I didn't come to take away a thing from you. I only came to rest until tomorrow."

My mother looked at him again from head to toe and I could see that she was warming to him.

"Don't do it, Mama."

"Is all right, Macky. I feel him is a good man."

"You may feel him is a good man, but I not taking any chances."

I ran to the kitchen and pulled the kitchen-knife from the drawer beside the sink. I hid it in the back of my pants and came out to the living room. The man walked inside the house and looked over at the crucifix my mother had on the wall and the picture of a white man with sheep and a shepherd's crook. It was almost as if he was sizing up the place to sell it.

"Jesus, is really you?"

"Yes, I am. But here is the mail that the postman left for you."

My mother stepped back. She wanted to believe him because all kinds of strange things have happened here in Westmoreland, and if those things could happen, then Jesus could come to our house. Still, she wasn't sure.

"If you really is Jesus, show me a sign."

"Are you turning a Pharisee on me, Darlene?"

"No, but if you going to spend the night here with me and my son, I have to know that we will be safe."

"All right. Come here."

My mother hesitated, but then Jesus came closer to her and whispered something in her ear. All of a sudden, my mother's eyes swelled up like when she heard that my father was arrested in Miami for murder. But this time, her eyes didn't look frightened.

"Macky, go clean up your room right now."

"But…"

"No buts, Macky. Listen to me. Jesus spending the night with us. He going sleep in your bed and you will sleep in my room. I will sleep on the sofa."

"No," said Jesus, "I will sleep on the sofa."

"Jesus," my mother said, "you in my house. You going sleep in Macky's room, Macky going sleep in my room, and I going sleep on the sofa. End of argument."

That's when I knew everything was over. Anytime my mother said, "End of argument," she wasn't going to change her mind. Everyone, including Jesus, had to obey.

I take one look at Jesus, *chupse,* and go to my room to clean it up. I picked up my clothes off the floor and stuffed them into a pillowcase. I dusted off the bed and made sure that the sheets were tucked under the edges the way my father taught me.

When I came back to the living room, my mother was sitting with Jesus by the dining table and they were talking softly to each other. My mother was crying.

She wiped her eyes and looked up at me.

"Macky, lock up the house for me. I have to get to the hotel early tomorrow, so I'm going to fix up the room for you. Show Jesus you room."

Jesus waited for her to get up and he followed me to my room.

"I'm sorry this happened. I never meant to kick you out of your own room."

"You lie. For if you were Jesus, you would know everything."

"Macky, I'm a man just like you."

That was all he said and he went into my room. And that was

when the doubts came back. If he really was Jesus, he should have known that he was taking away the best bed in the house – the bed Uncle Garfield (my mother says I shouldn't call him that) bought for me when he gave this house to us.

Now I had to sleep on a rickety old bed. I was a light sleeper because since my father went to jail five years ago, I've been the only one who has been protecting my mother and keeping her safe. Sometimes I wished that Uncle Garfield was my father because he's done more for me that my father who is going live until he dies in prison.

I kept my clothes on and pulled the kitchen knife from the back of my waist before I got in the bed. Jesus or no Jesus, if I heard a sound coming from anywhere near my mother in the living room, so help me, if he had made one wrong move to hurt my mother, Jesus or no Jesus, I would have stabbed him that Saturday night.

I pulled the covers over my chest and moved the knife closer to my heart.

★

The next morning I woke up in a cold sweat. What if he really was Jesus? I was going to have a whole heap of explaining and begging to do.

I brushed my teeth, washed my face, and then checked the sofa where my mother had slept. It was cold. She had probably left before daybreak. I went over to my room. The bed had been made, and the Bible that belonged to my grandfather on my father's side was between the pillows.

The light by the bed had been left on and when I went to turn it off, I saw Jesus praying under the mango tree my father had planted. I didn't want to interrupt him with my questions, so I went and made myself some breakfast.

After I'd eaten it, I looked out the window. Jesus was still praying. I washed the dishes, dried the dishes, and put them in the cupboard and he was still praying. Someone had to stop him, for I needed to confess.

As I walked out the back door, Jesus looked up and he saw me.

He was wearing my father's clothes, but I didn't say anything because if he was really Jesus, then he could do anything he wanted.

"Jesus?"

But before I could say anything, he put his fingers on his lips.

"It's all right, Macky. Why are you always in a rush? Take it easy, man. Take it easy."

He rose, brushed the dirt off my father's pants, and looked down the hill to the sea. The fishermen, who had been up before dawn, were pulling their boats onto the sand and hanging their nets on the sea grapes.

"Come, let us walk."

"Where are we going?"

"To see Garfield Holding. He and I have some business."

Uncle Garfield knew Jesus? Everybody had said that he was a big man, but now I knew.

I closed the back door, but by the time I turned around, Jesus was already out the gate. He wasn't walking fast, but I could tell he was on a mission. I locked the gate behind me, and ran to catch up with him.

We were about half way down the hill when we met Captain McKenzie who lives at the top of the hill. From his house, you can see all of Negril and all the land his family used to own. It was because of him that many of my friends have to walk miles and miles, as far as to Montego Bay, because they're afraid of having sex with their own sisters.

Captain McKenzie was out for his "morning constitutional," and he was frightened when he saw me and Jesus. He hadn't spoken to me since the morning I was walking with Uncle Garfield and Captain McKenzie said to him, "Garfield, I hear your friend is in prison. What you going do when him turn battyman?"

And Uncle Garfield said, "The same thing I always do. Send them to see you daddy. He's never complained to me."

Jesus just nodded as we passed each other on the narrow path. My eyes met the captain's when we both turned around to look at each other, but Jesus kept on walking and enjoying the sea breeze rustling through the breadfruit trees.

When we reached the bottom of the hill, we saw Miss Mabel at the crossroads. She was probably coming home from the rum bar and all the church sisters, who were coming in the opposite direction, were passing her as if they didn't know her. I could barely recognize her – the rum had twisted her face. We rarely go to church, only Easter and Christmas, but when we do go, she's usually up there in the choir, singing her life away in every note, and then falling asleep near the end of the sermon and showing the men in the congregation the other kingdom.

"You are a very rude boy," said Jesus, "but you will grow out of it. Now hurry up and make yourself useful."

Just as he said that, Miss Mable looked as if she was going to fall and Jesus ran and caught her. She would have done some serious damage to her headcup if he hadn't caught her.

"Jesus! Thank you," she said out of habit.

"Is all right, Mable. Is all right."

It was like she sobered up.

"Jesus. Jesus. Is really you? Is really you?"

"Yes, Mable."

"I so glad to see you. I so glad to see you," and she hugged him. "How long you staying this time?"

"I don't know. You behaving yourself?"

"You know how it go, Jesus. You say we must love our enemy and white rum is my enemy, so I only doing what you say."

"You too bad, Mable."

She leaned on Jesus' shoulder and Jesus kotched her on a boulder under a star-apple tree.

"Take some shade here and let the white rum come out of your system."

"All right, Jesus. Walk good. Walk good."

We left Miss Mable fanning herself with a wet handkerchief she always kept in her bosom. We headed west at the crossroad and turned down the lane that led to Uncle Garfield's house.

His house was not as big as Captain McKenzie's, but what it lacked in size, he made up with paint. Everything in the yard was painted. If he could have painted the two pit bulls that greeted us at the wrought iron gate, he would have done so.

Jesus knocked on the gate.

"What you want?"

"I've come to see Garfield."

"Man, guwaan bout your business. Mr. Garfield don't see nobody on Sunday."

"He will see me. Tell him that a special friend is here to see him."

"What you trying to say? Mr. Garfield don't have no special friend. Man, you better move before I shoot you."

"I wouldn't do that. But I'm telling you, if you don't tell him, he's going to be upset with you."

A small peephole opened, and then closed. Footsteps scurried towards the house and then more footsteps towards us.

"Put way the dawgs! Put way the dawgs!"

The gate opened and Uncle Garfield came out to greet us. His bodyguard, Tony, a vicious little man with scars all over his face, nicknamed "Take Nuff Life", hovered near him.

"Is all right, Tony. Go get yourself a Guinness."

Tony spat on the floor and went back inside the house.

"Jesus, how you doing? Long time no see."

Uncle Garfield, dreadlocked and thin, went and hugged Jesus – though he looked more as if he was patting Jesus down. He gave me a little slap across my face.

"Macky, you getting big. Your father would be proud."

Uncle Garfield pointed over to his verandah that was painted in lime green and overlooked a small private beach. Except for the paint, it was the kind of place that I hoped one day to be able to live in with my mother. He had freshly cut bougainvilleas and hibiscus in vases on mahogany tables surrounded by wicker chairs. The terrazzo floor looked as if it had been scrubbed a million time because it shone like a Marcus Garvey twenty-dollar coin.

"What I can do you for, Jesus?"

Garfield sat in the largest wicker chair and motioned for us to sit. He fanned himself with some *Watchtower* magazines that had been pushed under the gate. Tony loved to read them.

I waited until they were both seated before I sat.

"You know why I am here, Garfield."

"Where's you manners, Jesus. Youthman, you want a lemon-ade? Or a Red Stripe?"

Uncle Garfield was offering me a Red Stripe? I was moving up in the world with Jesus by my side.

"No, it's all right, Uncle Garfield. I'm all right."

"Cool. Now, Jesus, you sure you want the boy to hear this?"

"He's the reason why I'm here."

Well, I'm sorry to disappoint you, Jesus, to make you come all this way, but it's no deal."

"No deal? Why not?"

"Well, Jesus, after you left the last time, I really start to think about everything. And I like my life how it is. Look around you. Look at all this. Most people in Jamaica would kill to have a house like this." He laughed. "And you know what make this; you know what make this, Jesus?"

"Tell me."

"Money make this, Jesus. Money."

"I know that. But you said."

"Don't mind what I said. No deal."

"You begged me."

"So what?"

"Three times."

"Mmmm, and...?"

"Garfield, three times you begged and promised me. Three times. When you got shot and you were about to die, you said, 'Jesus, help me,' and I did. The second time when you thought you caught AIDS from the tourist woman, you said, 'Jesus, don't make it happen to me.' Nothing happened. The third time when you knew you were going to jail and you said, 'Jesus, I don't want to go to jail. I don't want to go to jail. I will do anything not to go to jail'. You said that, not me."

"So?"

"And when you found out that Macky's father was going to prison for your crime, you said that in five years you would give him all the money and follow me. I am here. To collect."

"I give him a house and him mother work down at my hotel. What more you want?"

"Justice."

"Well, just like two thousand years ago, Jesus. It not happening today. You might as well go home."

"Don't talk you him like that!" I said

"Sit yourself down, boy. Big man talking here."

Jesus looked at me and I sat down.

"Let me tell you something, Jesus. I realize that you are a big man and everything, but I also know that you can't do a thing to me. And even if you could, I don't care. Right now, me is forty years old. I outlive you by seven years and I outlive all my friends, some of them by twenty years. So what you can do to me? What? You think I'm afraid of you? Money is my God. Money take care of me better than you. I can do anything I want because I have money – even buy a lawyer so I won't go to jail. I'm not afraid of you any more, so you can do what you want."

"I've never told anyone to be afraid of me."

Uncle Garfield turned to me and said apologetically, "Now you see why I don't respect him, Youthman. Jesus soft."

Uncle Garfield was right.

"All right then. If that is you answer, then we are going."

"You sure you don't want a lemonade? Is a long walk back and I don't want you to think you left empty handed."

"No, Garfield. We will see ourselves out."

"I can't believe you!" I screamed and I ran towards Garfield, but Jesus held me back.

"Because of you I dropped out of school and now I can't get a job. You mashed up my life!"

Tony came running out of the house with his gun drawn. Two shirtless bodyguards came running out after him.

"Everything all right, boss?"

Garfield smiled.

"Everything irie. Them was just leaving. Right, Jesus?"

Jesus held my hands and I walked out of Garfield's house. The bodyguards escorted us through the gates and I spat on the sidewalk. Now I was walking faster than Jesus.

By the time I got to the crossroads, Miss Mable had already left. Jesus walked up to the boulder and looked around the trunk of the star-apple tree.

"You go on up to the house. I'm going to get Miss Mable. She's probably at the bar."

"I can't believe you let him talk to you like that. I can't believe you let him get away with all of that – putting my father in jail for him."

"I didn't put your father in jail. He chose that because he thought Garfield would help you better than he could."

"And when Garfield broke his promise, you let him get away with that!"

"What did you want me to do?"

"Burn him up with hell fire. Strike him down with lightning like they say in the Bible!"

"Macky, I know you don't know me too well, but listen to me. You need to let go of your anger, or you will either kill yourself or somebody."

"And? What difference does it make? You don't do anything. People killing people, doing all kinds of terrible things and all you can do is look. Do something! Make them fear you."

"I never told anybody to be afraid of me. I've told them that I was their brother."

"Great. So what use are you to me?"

"None."

"So why be good, then?"

"To save yourself."

He walked over to the boulder and then looked out at the sea. He patted the place where Miss Mable had sat and looked down towards the bar. Jesus wept.

"You all right, Jesus?"

"I'm all right. The things we do to ourselves, eh. Let me tell you if anyone burns in hell-fire or goes to hell, it's they who put themselves there. Now, you go on up to the house. I'm going to get Mable. She'll come with me this time."

And with that, Jesus left me by the crossroads and I continued up the hill towards my house. When I got home, I headed straight to my room, got the Bible, and began reading to see if what he was telling me was true.

I was up to Leviticus when I heard the knocking on the door, and, by the time, I got out of my room, Jesus was with my mother helping her with the food she had brought from the hotel.

My mother laid out the food on the table and although my mother begged him to say grace, Jesus refused and said she was the woman of the house. For the first in a long time, my mother and I sat down and talked.

"Your father might soon be coming back here."

"Might?" I said.

"You see how these things work. You never can tell. People tell me they are going to do things, and then they forget or back away. That why I'm saying it might happen. But I have a good feeling about this. Believe it or not, your father's lawyer might come forward."

When Jesus said this I knew he had to be lying. Or it had to be a miracle.

My mother gasped.

"What?"

"Yes, his conscience got to him, but we will see."

My mother clasped Jesus' hand and mine. She then broke the bread and some of the fried fish that the fishermen had given her and we laughed and talked all the way into the night.

At around ten o'clock, I was getting tired and so was my mother.

"Well, I don't know about the two of you, but I have busy day ahead of me. Sleep tight the two of you."

"Goodnight, Mama."

"Goodnight, Mama," said Jesus, and he made a face at me. Jesus was mocking me?

My mother went to sleep on the sofa and I went to my room. I left Jesus in the dining room cutting a piece of hard dough bread and licking his fingers.

"Thick and rich."

I closed the door and went straight into bed under the covers. I started to go over the day in my head, but before I got up where I'd met Captain McKenzie, I was falling asleep. Then for the first time in my life, I went to sleep without worrying. I slept and dreamt. Dream and slept without a worry. Jesus was outside my door.

A JAMAICAN CHRISTMAS STORY

Terry knew it had been a bad idea from the start, but this was where his journey had taken him. He looked down at the flat tire on his battered car and was about to curse in the tongue of his Gaelic youth when he felt the cold barrel of a revolver against the back of his skull.

"White boy, don't move."

He had been standing there looking at the car, and had been caught up in the refrain of Handel's "Messiah". Someone from one of the yards had turned up the volume on the radio as if to offer a benediction, to drown out the noise of pot and pans, the shouts and screams of women in the tenements, and the occasional pop-pop of a revolver punctuating the hallelujahs that mocked the twilight gloom of August Town.

"If you move, you dead."

He had asked for this he supposed. Sooner or later he would have been spotted – the whitest man in Jamaica in one of the blackest ghettoes in Kingston. He felt naked.

Was this was how his life was going to end – staring at a broken down car in a urine-soaked lane? But to die in stagnant pools of sewage at the side of the road? Where was the endless green of Ireland? He had left one war and stepped right into the middle of another. Two countries, two islands that resembled each other in so many ways: cramped bars, fratricidal battles, big hearts, and terrible tempers.

Lines the nuns had beaten into him in high school came back to his lips with bile:

We had fed the heart on fantasies,
The heart's grown brutal from the fare,

More substance in our enmities
Than in our love

He had chosen this. Somewhere in the midst of this insanity, the killings, the blood, something had to make sense. When Terry reached out to his brothers and sisters in these killing fields, he felt a real connection. Human to human. That union couldn't be forged or faked – that was *his* good news.

He had fallen in love with this country where, down in the bush, people still used the beautiful language of the *King James Bible* with words like, "peradventure" instead of the new words like "shotta".

Anger rushed through his body, but he quickly calmed himself. He did not want to die with a mortal sin in his mind, but wasn't it a mortal sin that brought him here in the first place, that made everything he had touched a failure?

He quelled these thoughts and concentrated on what was happening to him in the moment. He began whispering to himself, "Hail Mary, Mother of God, pray for us sinners, now, and at the hour of our death," and then he broke off. He couldn't go on. It wasn't right. He knew whatever he said would be heard – he was estranged from God.

"I don't have much money. I am… was a priest."

"Don't lie, white boy, you about to dead."

"I don't lie."

That was one sin he knew was not in his character, yet it was his biggest fault. He should have lied to the bishop, kept everything hush-hush, and remained in his parish, but he couldn't. He should have lied when Denise asked him if he loved her. But he didn't.

"Turn around."

"No."

He did not want to see the gunman's face. He knew if he was to survive he should avoid doing anything that would identify the gunman in front of him. He dropped his eyes to the dust.

The gunman tapped him on his head with the butt of the revolver.

"Is me have the gun, you know. Is me in charge here, so turn round."

"No."

He wasn't going to give the gunman the pleasure of humiliating him. If he died, then God could add pride to his list of sins that was growing day by day, hour by hour.

"Don't make me have to shoot for you to turn around."

He decided to take pride off God's list and turned in the dust, but kept his eyes on the ground.

"Look at me."

Terry stared at his feet. He would not look up.

"Father, look at me."

The word, *Father*, sounded almost obscene coming from the lips of this man who was about to kill him, but Terry raised his eyes.

The man was about six feet and very muscular. He probably didn't need the gun to rob people. He could have robbed them with his bare hands.

"Do you know me, Father?"

The word weighed heavy, like a huge stone with which he was now burdened and would carry for the rest of his life.

"No, son."

He would have to learn to stop saying the word 'son' in that way. It was a life he was leaving behind.

"Father McDougall, it's me, Rupert."

Terry still didn't recognize him. Thirty years ago when the war had been controlled by politicians, he had requested to be assigned to Jamaica – a chance to practice the liberation theology that inspired him. When he first came to August Town, he'd met resistance from some of the local *massives*, but when they realized that he was there to save souls by feeding and clothing the poor, they "lowed" him. During those years, he had baptized many of these boys, some of whom then took first communion, presided over a few of their marriages, and prayed at many more funerals as they were lowered into the ground.

That was how he'd met Denise. The hours of counsel and comfort he'd given her after the death of her husband had become something else. At first, he denied all attraction and tried to bury his feelings in their differences of age, class, and colour. And when all that failed, he resorted to his final defence – St Augustine and the gap between his education and hers.

"I don't recognize you, Rupert."

Rupert began peeling off the tam and the rag that covered his face.

"No, no, no! Don't do that."

Terry knew he was dead now and tried to muster the courage to continue the "Hail Mary".

Rupert tucked his gun away in the back of his pants waist and patted Terry on the shoulder.

"Is all right, Father. Is all right... What happen to you car?"

"Flat tire."

"Let me help you. You have a jack?"

"Yes, in the trunk."

"Give me the keys."

Terry, although still cautious, threw the keys to him. Rupert opened the trunk and pulled out the jack and the spare tire. He slipped the jack under the car and began cranking the lever. Terry tried to help, but Rupert wouldn't let him.

"You just stand up there, Father, and let a pro do this."

Rupert was right. In a matter of minutes, he had taken off the flat tire and replaced the flat with the spare.

"You really are a pro."

"Long time me doing this."

"And how long you been a gunman?"

Terry knew he shouldn't have asked, but he had to. Rupert had recognized him and until he'd given up his vestments, he would be the priest for the area.

"I used to do this, but I stopped about ten Christmases ago when you got me out of jail. You remember now?"

"No."

"My big brother was charged with murder and the police hold him, me and my little brother for questioning. My mother nearly dead when she hear that the three of we was going to be in jail for Christmas. Them was going murder we in jail with licks if we never testify against me brother."

It was slowly coming back. Terry looked into the darkness outside the dim pool of light from the one electric pole covered with posters of an Xmas dancehall: *Sergeant Satta and Juta Congo in control. Security tight, tight, tight.*

139

"But, Father, you come to the jail with a lawyer and you get me and my little brother out. You make sure that everything was all right and gave us a Christmas dinner when we never have nothing."

"I'm beginning to remember. What happened to your brother?"

"Dead."

"How?"

"How else him to dead? Gun shot."

Rupert's eyes had the stare of a man who'd seen death many times: hands clutching feebly at the concrete sidewalk, legs tucked under the body, parted slightly to form a K.

"So why are you doing this now?"

"Get fired. The boss come a month ago and lean under the car me was fixing and say him have to let me go."

"Just like that?"

"Just so."

"But you're a good worker."

"I know that and him know that. But him have high overhead, so him let me go like me don't have baby mother to feed. Things got bad in the house between me and my woman and the children wanted some food, so me decide to try me hand at the gun business again."

"So, you were going to rob me?"

"Yes, Father. But this is a sign I have to find something else to do. I don't know what, but God only give so many chances you know."

"God gives us as many chances as we need."

"How you can say that? Look around you. And how come you not wearing you collar?"

The collar was the last thing he had torn off his neck when he left the bishop's office and came back to tell Denise about his plans. It still burned in his pocket.

"I'm not a priest any more."

"Don't lie, Father."

"I don't lie."

Terry didn't know where the conversation was heading, but he motioned to Rupert and they sat on the ground with their backs against the fence, watching the mongrels dig through the ruins of the burnt-down grocery store. The evening star, Venus, blinked through the clouds. Terry told Rupert the whole long story of how he met Denise after her husband had died from sickle cell and all his evasions of pretending not to love her.

"But you know, what made me fall in love with her was when she spoke about her relationships with God and how she *knew*, not believed, but *knew* she was going to get through her hardships. God for her wasn't someone in the sky, but a real presence in her life, someone with whom she had a relationship and with whom she wanted to deepen the relationship. She ministered to me. She taught me. That was when I realized I wanted to spend the rest of my life with her. All that I had learned from books, all that I had read, Denise was just speaking from her heart. She had put all my homilies of faith to shame. So I said to hell with it!"

"Easy, Father. Any way, she sound like she is a good woman. I say keep her."

"She cost me my collar."

"Sound like the collar was too heavy."

"You may be right."

"And how old is she, Father?'

"Thirty-eight."

"And you?"

"Next year, I'm fifty."

"For a ghetto woman, even if she is Catholic, that's more than two lifetimes. You right, she have a whole heap to teach you. Father, you can either go with what you believe or with what you know. I say go with what you know."

"You're right, son. You're right. So, what are you going to do now?"

"I don't know. I only know my baby mother want some food for the children."

Terry went to his pocket to give Rupert some money, as if he too didn't have a baby mother to care for.

"No, keep it, Father. I will find something."

"No, you take it. If you're going hold up someone else, then take it."

"No, Father. Me done with the gun business tonight."

"What about tomorrow?"

"Don't know, Father. Me have to live one day at a time."

"Promise me no more gun business."

Terry stuck out his hand with the bills and shook them.

"Promise me."

Rupert took the money.

"I promise, Father."

The word pressed against his chest like the ragged edge of a stone and bruised his heart.

"I don't know if you should still call me Father."

"It don't matter what them do or say about you, you will always be Father McDougall to me."

Rupert rose to his feet and helped Terry out of the dust. He walked with him over to the car, opened the door, and handed him the keys.

"So what you going do now, Father?"

"The bishop says he can get me a job down at St George's to coach the football team."

"I never know you was a baller, Father?"

They stared at each other, and then laughed.

"I never mean it that way, Father."

"I never took it that way, but I guess I will have to get used to it. Father McDougall, the baller from August Town."

It hurt to say it, but he saw the humour. He cranked up the engine and it made a grinding sound.

"I'll come down to the church if you're still there tomorrow and fix that engine. You need to get out of here fast. It not safe for you any more."

"How much you going charge me for fixing it?"

"For you, Father, nothing."

Terry put the car in first gear and waved goodbye. Rupert pulled down the shirt over the gun in his back and waved.

As he shifted the car into second gear, Terry checked the rear view-mirror, but Rupert had already disappeared into the darkness leaving only the curses and the benedictions, the hoots and the hosannas of the darkened lanes of August Town.

SISTER FAYE
AND THE DREADLOCKED VAMPIRE

It had been three weeks since the last time, and I could tell Sister Faye was worried when she stumbled into my room that Saturday morning. It was eleven o'clock and I was still in bed when she came over to my room and looked through the window at the garden. She shook her head and scratched the inside of her thigh. She looked thinner than usual, pale and drawn.

"M-M-M-Mosquitoes still biting you at night? I don't know how them getting inside your room."

I wanted to soften her up because I thought she was going to punish me for lingering in bed.

"You want me to rub some sinkle bible on it for you?"

"To tell you the truth, Walter," Sister Faye said, "I don't know how them getting inside the room because I lock the window. Thanks for asking though, but where them biting me you can't touch. Maybe when you grow up," and she rub her hand over my head and smiled.

Now I know some slack-minded people, like my best friend Tony, might think she was trying to get me excited, but it isn't like that. My mother sent me away from Kingston to live with Sister Faye in Westmoreland to get me away from bad influences. She was afraid that I was going to become a Rasta. That's what her latest boyfriend kept telling her, and I never made things easier for my mother.

Like one day during Bible knowledge class, Father Owen (I went to an all-boys' Catholic school) caught me twirling my hair and he said, "I don't want any Rastas in this school. That sort of thing is not permitted."

Now, I wasn't thinking about being a Rasta or anything like

that when I was twirling my hair. I was looking at the thumb on my right hand and wondering if I'd got an infection. I'd bitten my fingernails until they'd bled and torn off a piece of the skin at the side of my thumb. It was swollen and I couldn't tell my mother about it because she was only going to say, "How many times I tell you not to bite your fingernail?"

The thumb had pus and that was what worried me. But Father Owen was sure that I was planning to become a Rasta, so he called my mother. Father Owen was always telling us, "One swallow does not a summer make," so why not, "One twirl of a lock does not a Rasta make"? Who would want to turn Rasta anyway. You can't eat pork, beef, or meat of any kind. And I love beef.

I begged my mother not to send me away, but she wouldn't listen to me. Her boyfriend was behind it. I couldn't understand it. If as Father Owen says, "Blood is thicker than water," then why was my mother doing this?

As I said, she sent me down to the country to live with her cousin, Sister Faye (who even my mother agreed was a little weird), but she was the only person my mother said she could trust me with. She was hoping some of Sister Faye's godly ways could rub off on me.

Sister Faye and my mother grew up together, and ever since Sister Faye was nine years old she'd been having visions of my great-grandfather. That's why she was still in the same house where her father and grandfather died. Every Sunday morning, before she went to church, she'd have a conversation with my great-grandfather – tell him about everything that was happening in the village.

So for the past nine months I've been living with Sister Faye and going to church with her every Sunday morning at Mt. Airy Church of God. One thing I can say about Sister Faye's services is that they're very funny. All the congregation sings, jumps, and gets into the spirit. Some of the women get so excited when they start to speak in tongues, the men have to rush to cover them up when they fall to the ground.

But two months ago, the regular pastor, Brother Ezekiel, died of a heart attack. Sister Faye took it really badly. Brother Ezekiel, who was like a father to her, was a sprightly old man, and was still making his daily rounds to the congregation right until he died. Some Sunday nights when I would pass by the chapel, the light would still be on and I could see him working. The next morning he'd be up before me, and I'd see him coming back from Darliston saying, "Early to bed, early to rise," while I stumbled all the way to school.

After he died, a new preacher, Brother Belnavis, took over and things started to change. He brought a whole new set of teachings. Sisters could now wear pants and jewellery. Brother Belnavis himself wore a stubby three-inch crucifix of solid gold. He changed the services from only Sundays to Mondays, Wednesdays, and Fridays. The collection plate was always full.

At first, Sister Faye, didn't like the change. But when the poor, hard-working sisters, whose baby fathers were slaving in Miami and sending back every penny, started to tell Sister Faye about how when Brother Belnavis laid his hands on them, they felt the power of the Holy Spirit rush through their bodies, from the bottom of their bellies down to their toes, Sister Faye started to go to every meeting after she finished working as a cook at the *Hog Heaven Hotel*. On Saturday mornings, she could barely lift herself out of the bed to eat breakfast. And for the past two Saturdays, Brother Belnavis had been coming over to lay his hands on her and I didn't like it. Sister Faye strip down her clothes to as far as modesty allow (but enough for Brother Belnavis to be able to see the birthmark on the side of her belly), then she kneels and he stands in front of her, puts his hands on her head, and squeezes her. Sometimes he stood there for ten to twenty minutes pressing her head to his body so hard that when he left she still had the mark of his belt-buckle on her cheek.

Last week, all of a sudden, he started jerking around and saying, "Malaka, malvorium, malusa." She dropped on the bed and fluttered around, her arms waving in the air like something shocked her, like a chicken that got its head chopped off. Then she passed out cold. Was a good thing he only did this at the house. If he did it at the church, I would have to drag her down Mt. Airy to the house, and that was not something I wanted to do. Sister Faye was not a fat woman. She's a good looking, brown woman with long black hair, firm hips, slightly bowed legs, but she weigh just a little bit too much. But that and a whole heap of other things were beginning to change.

Ever since Brother Belnavis took over the church, she'd been giving into her single vice. Sister Faye loved to wear a chain her only boyfriend gave to her before she converted, at sixteen, with her father to the Church of God.

Her father, my Uncle Alvin, had always been jealous of the boys who came to visit her, and after their conversion, he wouldn't allow any man who was not a member of the church near the house. He kept a whip in the parlour just in case he had to use it. That went on for twenty years until he died.

After he died, Sister Faye used to put on her chain before service, look at herself in the mirror for quite some minutes, then take off the chain and put it on the night table beside her bed. Afterwards, she would go out into the garden and talk with my great-grandfather. But she made the mistake of telling Brother Belnavis about these conversations. He said it was all down to demons and he had to drive them out. It was the same demons, he said, had killed a dozen chickens that belonged to Sister McDonald, (a white woman from Sav-la-Mar who was getting paler and paler every week), drained their blood, and scattered the bodies over her yard. It was his mission, he said, to clean up all the nastiness and devilisms that were happening in the village.

Brother Belnavis didn't much approve of Sister McDonald because she only came to church on Easter Sunday and Christmas. Her family had once owned all the land in Struie, but now she was rarely seen outside her house since she was jilted by her boyfriend forty years ago. All these years she'd survived on her teacher's pension and her house, which was once the pride of the village, had fallen into disrepair – a disgrace in a town full of disgrace. Brother Belnavis had hissed that she was a good-for-nothing woman who was as mad as she was lazy.

At first, I liked it when he came over, because Sister Faye was always happy to see him. She even wore the ankle bracelet he bought for her, and it was good she finally had a little joy in her life. If I'd been a woman I think I would have liked him too. Even though he wore black most of the times, he was a sharp dresser – the total opposite of my mother's boyfriend who wore coffee-stained T-shirts, grubby stone-washed blue jeans, and second-hand Nike sneakers, trying to look American. Brother Belnavis's shoes were real leather and his silk suits never had a speck of dust on them, even though he travelled up and down the country roads of Westmoreland in his old, but well-maintained, Ford Cortina. And he could fix things. He fixed Sister Faye's toaster and her fridge. He fixed her electric grill and her electric rollers. He could fix anything electrical. But one night, when he came here unexpectedly, and I was helping Sister Faye out of her girdle, the man took after me like a rat in a barrel of molasses. After that, the man wouldn't stop sneaking up on me and haunting my every move.

First, he got my friend Tony expelled from school. They'd hired brother Belnavis to teach biology and religious knowledge after Brother Ezekiel died, and one day, after we'd studied the book of Genesis, Tony went out to the toilets and spray-painted on the wall: "Free will is a Bitch."

When the janitor saw the graffiti, he started cursing a whole string of bad words. He said he was tired of all the slackness around the school and he wasn't going to clean it up. The Principal brought in the usual suspects, Larry and Eric, (they were always in the toilets at the same time), but they said it was Tony. They even told the principal where the spray-can was and showed him some copies of *Playboy* Tony had brought to school. I was shocked they had squealed on him. Everyone knew that although he was in the same class with us, Tony was the oldest boy in the school. And at six feet three and one hundred and ninety pounds, he was the biggest boy in the football team. He had a scar over his left eye, pimples all over his face, and a full beard when the rest of us only had Spanish needles on our chins. People thought he was the meanest boy in the school, but they were all wrong – no one had a softer heart. Tony would never knowingly hurt anyone or pick a fight, but no one wanted to test him.

I became his best friend because I helped him with his math, so he would finally be able to get out of fifth form. Our friendship grew after Tony told me he, too, had been sent down to the country – to live with his grandmother – so that his mother could work in Miami. His mother was always shipping him off to live with relatives. Sometimes people he didn't even know.

But then Brother Belnavis started in on Tony and said what a bad influence he was and how he couldn't teach in a school with a boy like that.

"Abomination, fornication, and sin," he cried when he saw the copy of *Playboy* and picked it up with his forefinger and thumb. "The stench of thy sin reaches all the way to heaven. Repent, I say, you nasty, nasty, nasty boy."

Brother Belnavis told the principal it was either Tony or him. Tony was kicked out of school.

Now it wasn't that Tony was bad, he was just full of life. He would do things that nobody else would do. He was fearless. He was the only boy who could climb up into a naseberry tree full of wasps and pick the fruit without getting stung. I couldn't do that. I hate wasps. But one day Tony talked me into climbing up a guinep tree full of wasps. We were eating some of the sweetest guineps, popping the fleshy little balls in our mouths when Tony decided he wanted to pee. He pulled out his puppy and peed on a wasps' nest.

The wasps took after us and stung us all over. They were all over Tony, but even as they were stinging him, he was laughing. Some even stung him on his puppy and it swelled up as big as my arm. But he never seemed to mind. For a whole week he went down by the river where the girls used to wash their clothes, and he would take off all his clothes and wade in the water with his big puppy steering through the water.

"What made you do it?" I asked as we were sitting down by the side of the river and watching the dragonflies race over the water.

"To see what would happen next."

"But you had to know what was going to happen next, that we would get stung."

"Not every time," he said. "Not every time."

Brother Belnavis got rid of Tony and then came after me. He started to follow me around so I couldn't do anything without him knowing. On the day before Tony left, we decided to get a few Cadbury's chocolate bars from Mr. Chang's grocery store. "The Crissers", girls from St. Theresa's, Tony explained, loved chocolate, especially Cadbury's. And although he suspected the chocolate made his pimples worse, he couldn't resist the temptation. We were going to unwrap the golden foil wrapped around the pure, milk chocolate in front of their eyes, and see if we could entice them to slip out of their starched, white uniforms.

The plan was that Tony would break a bottle outside the door and when Mr. Chang went outside to see what had happened, I would lift a few chocolate bars and put them in my knapsack.

As I lifted the chocolate, Brother Belnavis grabbed me by my neck.

"The Bible says, 'A foolish son is a grief to his father and bitterness to her that bare him.'"

He dragged me in front of Mr. Chang and made me apologize.

"The two of them must be playing with themselves," Mr. Chang said and cut his eye at me. But I didn't feel too bad, for I really didn't consider it stealing. I worked at Mr. Chang's store and I know he pays only fifty cents for the chocolate, but he charges two dollars. I was going to leave the fifty cents on the counter before Brother Belnavis grabbed me. Mr. Chang had been overcharging people for years now. So who's thiefing who?

Brother Belnavis told Sister Faye what had happened and I could tell she was disappointed with me. She just shook her head and went upstairs to her room. She said she wished Brother Belnavis would lay his hands on me and he did. The man boxed me so hard over my head I saw wasps coming at me all day.

I had to watch myself. I couldn't tell Sister Faye anything because she wouldn't believe me. She'd ask me why I wanted to disgrace a man of God, so I kept everything to myself. I didn't even laugh out loud when he claimed that the wooden crucifix embedded on the cover of his Bible was made from the splinters of the Cross. I put my head under the desk so he wouldn't see me laughing. I remembered that Father Owen saying that so many splinters of the Cross had been sold to simpletons that if all the splinters were put together, they could build a million of Noah's Arks.

But Brother Belnavis was proud of his Bible, which had been given to him, he explained to us, by his mentor, the great Pastor Witherspoon, and he would carry it with him everywhere – especially when he went to visit the sisters of the church. He would wave it around, touch the cover and begin swaying and talking in tongues. It was all too much for a young Catholic boy like me.

When Sister Faye told me he was coming over again that afternoon, I planned to be far from that place. I didn't want to be any part of that madness.

"Brother Belnavis say he want to pray for you this afternoon."

"It-It's all right. I will just go down by the river. Why can't he come early in the morning like Brother Ezekiel?"

"He's a busy man and he always sleeps late. But before you go, I going ask you to help me clean up the house. I always feel so drained after church service."

I helped her and it took us about three hours to clean the bathroom, the living room, and my room. It never used to be this hard, but since she's been praying so hard, the whole house is falling apart. Then we went upstairs and I helped her to clean her room and make her bed. It was when I was putting her water bottle under the bed, I saw the mango.

It was the sweetest, reddest Bombay mango and it was right in the middle of the tree. But wasps were all around it. It was ripe and ready for picking. With all those wasps around it, I was sure it didn't have any worms. Now if Tony had been there he would have just jumped through the window and we would be biting into the skin, letting the juice run all over our mouths and chewing down to the seed until the hairs stuck in our teeth. But Tony was gone. His mother had sent him off – to live with his aunt in St. Mary. I missed him.

I looked through the window and it was like the mango was calling my name. I walked over to the window and opened it.

"So why you don't stay and pray with me and Brother Belnavis?"

"I have big test this week."

"Liar," said the voice behind me. "You are from your father the Devil. He is a liar and the father of the lie.' He doesn't have any test. He wants to escape the judgment of heaven. That's why he's so frightened. That's why he stammers. He's afraid of the light that will reveal the iniquity of his secret sin that only he knows. But I know. I know!"

"Brother Belnavis," said Sister Faye, "so good to see you."

"Sister Faye, I greet you with the holy kiss of our Saviour."

"Sorry for the mess. I never expected you to be to here so early."

"The Lord is never too early or too late for his sheep."

Sister Faye sat on the bed and Brother Belnavis put his Bible on the night table beside it.

"Be off minion of Hades," he whispered to me, and just as Sister Faye closed her eyes, he boxed me over my head. I had another headache.

All I could do is go down by the riverside, hold my head, think about my mother, Sister Faye, and Tony and cry. I must have been crying for about an hour before I fell asleep. When I woke up, it was already ten o' clock at night.

I was feeling worried, so I hurried home. When I got there, Sister Faye had already collapsed on the bed and I came in through the door just as Brother Belnavis was going to lay his hands on her.

"Sh-Sh-She's all right?"

"Thy name is Legion," he shouted as he did something with his belt.

I could tell he was mad, so I ran back downstairs before he could catch me. I waited outside in the bushes. A few minutes later, he came out to the front door and he looked around. He didn't see me.

I waited until I saw the tail-lights of his Ford Cortina disappear down the road before I went inside.

Sister Faye was out cold and her clothes were all messed up. I rolled her under the sheets and covered her with a blanket. I was still so tired I forgot to lock the front door and just went to my room to get some sleep. Before I left her room, I noticed Brother Belnavis had left his Bible on the night table beside her bed. I knew he would come back before church service the next morning to get it, but that was the least of my worries. I wanted to get some sleep to get rid of the headache.

It was about eleven o'clock that night when I heard *spleng, splang spangalang lang* and it sounded like it was coming from Sister Faye's room. I rushed in to see what was happening.

When I got there, a breeze was blowing through the room, and all the sheets on her bed were pulled up. But Sister Faye was still asleep. I looked over to the right side of her bed and saw smoke coming from underneath the right side of the bed. I was rushing to put out the fire when I saw him.

"V-V-Vampire to raas!" was all I could say.

"Who leave this here?"

His hand was smoking with the mark of the crucifix. Thin, wiry and even handsome in a ragamuffin sort of way, his eyes were red and his teeth were as white as limestone.

"People must be more careful where they leave their things. That wasn't here the last time I called!"

He jumped away from the Bible.

I picked it up quickly and held it in front of me. He was afraid of it, and ducked when I held it in front of him.

"Careful with that Bible, youth man. You don't know what that thing is. So just put it down. I don't want to hurt you."

He sounded much older than he looked.

"And I don't want to hurt you either. S-S-S-So just get way from Sister Faye."

He backed away. He was trying to get to the window, but I blocked him and held up the Bible.

"Out of my may, youth man, this is deeper than you think."

"W-What you doing here? What you doing here in Sister Faye's room?"

"I don't like to bite man, so don't force me to. The last time I bite a man, hair start grow in me hand middle and my wife never like it."

His dreadlocks looked like they were on fire.

"You have a wife? So what you doing out here on a Saturday night?"

"Doing what all vampire do, sucking virgin blood."

"But why Sister Faye?"

"She remind me of a girl I used to know. But that was long ago."

He wrapped his dreadlocks with a rubber band and walked over to the door.

"Are you going kill her and take her away from me?"

"No, youth man. Me already have one woman. Me don't need no more crosses in me life," and he laughed to himself. "Your

Sister Faye is the last virgin left in Negril. The other virgin mad. You ever suck mad woman?"

I shook my head.

"Pray you never. Remember all them dead fowl that people find over that mad woman yard that people did think it was mongoose? Well, that was me." I could tell he was ashamed of himself. "That's what happen after you suck mad woman. After that you will suck anything, even fowl."

"And we did think it was mongoose."

"No, mad woman blood. And I don't want to go through that again."

"Well, I don't care if Sister Faye is the last virgin on the island, you're not going do anything to her. I don't want you coming back here." I held up the Bible, "Is not right."

I wasn't stammering.

"I know it not right. You think I don't know. You think I proud of this, of what I do, of what I've become?"

The way he said it, I really felt sorry for him. But before I put down the Bible I decided to ask him, "So how did you turn into a vampire? You born this way or what?"

Just as he was about to answer me, I heard, "Be not deceived 'for Satan himself keeps transforming himself into an angel of light.' "

"You!" said the vampire. "I know you was here, I could smell you hand all over this woman. Youth man, you lucky I get here in time. Is this man putting me out of business. If him keep it up, she really will be the last virgin in Jamaica and then I will be a dead vampire."

When Brother Belnavis heard that he opened up his shirt and pulled out his gold crucifix and pointed it at the vampire.

"You think your white Jesus can frighten me?"

The vampire's eyes grew red like a woodpecker's head.

Brother Belnavis looked at him and grabbed the Bible out of my hand. He jumped on the vampire and started to beat him with the Bible. Smoke was flying everywhere, and then he started to fiddle with his belt.

It was then I saw what he was doing all this time when he was laying his hands on Sister Faye's head. He had wires running up his arms and they were connected to a battery and some kind of booster inside his belt. He had been shocking Sister Faye. That was why she wasn't having her visions any more! He wasn't filled with the power of the Holy Spirit; it was the power of the Energizer!

"Join me, join me in the victory over Satan," Brother Belnavis shouted.

But when I saw the wires, I couldn't sit back and do nothing. I picked up the water bottle from under Sister Faye's' bed and waxed Brother Belnavis over the head with it. That shook him up and the vampire pushed him away.

Brother Belnavis got up all wobbly and when he saw the two of us standing there, he ran downstairs and closed the door behind him. Sister Faye was still asleep throughout all this bangarang.

The vampire eased by her bed, but before he left, he picked up her chain that had fallen on the ground. He looked at it, then placed it around her neck. He was so tender.

"You were the one who gave her that weren't you?"

"No," he said gruffly. "That was another man."

The vampire looked at my hands, nodded disapprovingly, and jumped through the window into the mango tree. As I was about to close the window, fearing that he'd awakened the wasps, a mango hit me in the chest and I caught it.

"Give thanks, youth man," said his voice out of the darkness. "You saved my life tonight. And don't worry, I won't bother Sister Faye any more."

"How you know I wanted this?"

"Desire come out of a man like heat out of a cat."

As he was about to jump down to the garden, I asked him. "You still haven't told me how you turn into a vampire."

"The rent-a-dread business don't good," he said. "White woman come from America and say she want a good time. So me show her around. Turn out she was the ex-wife of a Mormon. She make me do all kind of nastiness and then she bite me. Look at me now. Vampire. But stop worrying about those things. Not everything in this life is here to kill you! Stop bite your fingernail and live."

154

Then him jumped down out of the tree and disappeared.

"Hold on, what's your name?"

"Just call me Vampy," came the voice from the darkness.

Nobody ever saw Brother Belnavis after that night. Last Easter, Sister McDonald said he she saw him on a television show in Kingston and he was still laying his hands on the congregation. I didn't even know she had a television set. Brother Belnavis's replacement, Brother Michael, a short mousy man with a baldhead, who always wears flood length pants, just says prayers and sometimes even forgets to take the collections.

Sister Faye couldn't be happier. She and my great-grandfather are out there every Sunday morning and some mornings I think I can hear him laughing with her.

And I know Vampy comes back every now and then for a little suck.

But it's all right. As long as Vampy is around I know I'm safe from Brother Belnavis. Now I'm not afraid any more and many a Saturday night, it's me and Vampy, shoulder to shoulder, walking home in the dark.

MY JAMAICAN TOUCH

One of my biggest problems. Scratch that. My New Age, American friends tell me that there are no "problems" only "challenges".

One of my biggest challenges has been to control what my wife calls my "Jamaican touch". Similar to the "Midas touch" where everything that the king desired turned into gold, everything I touch (people, places or things) begins to speak and act Jamaican.

Now, as with everything else in life, my "Jamaican touch" is both a blessing and a curse. One of the blessings is that my wife, who is originally from Colombia, has really begun to understand me and my idiosyncrasies. But I was shocked when about ten years ago, she began to use words like *wet-up*. I swear, Jamaicans have an inborn sense of the transcendent because of the inordinate amount of words to which we have attached our own suffix "up": *Fix up, chop up, mash up, bus' up, bruk up, pretty up, dirty up, tear up, nice up,* and *tangle up.*

The first time I heard my wife say *wet-up*, I nearly burst out laughing. Nearly. We've been married for more than twenty years and unlike when we were newlyweds, I know what's good for me. I now keep my mouth shut. But when she asked me, "What sweet you so?" all I could do was to go outside and cut the grass so the lawnmower would drown the noise of my laughter. Learning to keep quiet, or running away if I fear laughing at the wrong time, has been a hard-won wisdom. But as my history teacher at Jamaica College once said to me before he gave me a detention, "Mr. Philp, discretion is the better part of valour."

So, the blessing, if used wisely, can lead to all kinds of bliss, marital and otherwise. But you have to be in control, especially when appliances begin to speak and act Jamaican. Not to boast, but anything, even the most stubbornly American or American with Chinese-made parts, in time, will yield to my touch. Sometimes I feel like the Borg in those *Star Trek* shows my friend, Leon, likes to watch: "Resistance is futile."

And all the appliances speak differently. The fridge is the nicest. Everything is "mi dear," and "How you feelin'?" "You hungry? You want something to eat?" whereas the toaster is all *fiah* and *claat this* and *claat that* with the dishwasher bawling, "Lawd, a mercy! Can't we all just get along?" and then starts to sing, "One Love, one heart. Let's get together and feel all right."

It's true I'm the only one who hears them and the one to whom they speak. Which is all right with me. Sometimes, I can't get along with some people and when I get home, it's always good to hear, "You looking tired, mi dear. I have just the right thing. Reach inside my freezer and get yourself a nice, cold beer."

Now in general, my fridge behaves in many ways like the sturdy Frigidaire we had when we lived in Mona Heights, Jamaica, and she is just as dependable. I use the pronoun "she" because as with all things female in Jamaica, you have to adopt certain behaviours in order to get what you want. In her case, you have to talk nicely with her if you want your ice cream to stay cold. With the male appliances, such as my toaster, you can't be *saaf*. You have to be willing, if necessary, *to chuck badness*, as one of our prime ministers once said, to get what you want. You *bax* it on its lever to get a piece of toast – and not burned – or you *bax* it again! And sometimes another *bax* for good measure. You have to be willing to *go Jamaican* on them. It's the only way they will respect you.

The touch, however, can lead to the most horrendous disasters. Just last week, I saw the worst side of the touch with my beloved fridge. She wouldn't even cool a glass of water for me.

At first, I didn't pay attention to her – which in hindsight may have made things worse. She was acting up, and I was busy with all kinds of Anancy business, so I really wasn't in any mood for her foolishness. I told her before I left the house, "You better have my ice cubes ready when I get home!" Well, she showed me. She also made me fear that I was beginning to lose my touch.

When I got home, she'd leaked water all over the floor and I had to mop it up before one of my *wutless* Red Stripe drinking friends slipped and fell. For if one of them broke an arm or leg, the next thing you know, they'd turn around and sue me. Everybody's changed since they've come to America, and some of them think, "*Bwai*, Geoffrey mus have money. Look how much book him publish."

One of them, Winston, who knew about my challenges with the fridge, whispered in my ear, "So, Geoff, why you don't buy a new one with all the royalties from you books?" I was going *to chuck some badness* on him, but changed my mind. I just kissed my teeth and said, "First, stop farting on my new sofa. And second, if ah buy a new one, she will become just as Jamaican as this one, so what good will that do me?" He thought about it for a minute. "You right," he said, and went back over to the sofa.

Things really got bad though when my wife, after watching *Desperate Housewives*, handed me a limp popsicle from the freezer and said, "Your fridge gone on strike. Fix her now. I'm not sitting through another episode of *Brothers and Sisters* like this!"

I didn't pay much mind; I was concentrating on challenges at work. But later that night when I was snuggling up to my wife, she said, "You fix the fridge yet?" I had to confess. "No, I haven't." And she said, "Well, you know what to do then."

So, I put on my pajamas and went downstairs, in the middle of the night, to talk to the fridge.

"Luscious (she likes it when I call her that)," I said, "what's wrong, baby?" She didn't feel like talking. I spent the whole night wiping her down and cleaning her gaskets. Still, she wouldn't talk. She just kept blowing hot air from her back. Next morning my wife found me sitting on a stool, half-asleep with the rag in my hand and mouth-water dripping down my pajama shirt.

My wife took the rag out of my hand, and cleaned the mouth-water off the side of the fridge. "She still not talking to you, eh?" I told her no. "Well, you better have her fixed by tonight because my mother is coming over tonight and you know how she feels about you already."

I still haven't converted my mother-in-law with my "Jamaican touch". Everything that I've tried so far has failed. She spent a lot of time in New York before she came to Florida, so I think this is why she's been able to resist. She is mortified by my interest in Anancy and Rastafari. She feels I have led her daughter away from the true Church, which according to her is "Roman, Catholic, and Apostolic!"

I spent the whole morning talking to Luscious. Nothing worked. Even when I opened her door, she wouldn't even turn on her light. It wasn't until ten in the morning that I got a slight hum out of her. Then, I had to call in sick because I realized I was making some progress.

Luscious and I watched *Dr. Phil* and *The View* together and, by the time *Oprah* rolled around, she was ready to talk.

I took the toaster and the blender to another room so they wouldn't hear. I didn't feel like *baxing* them any more. If they overheard and word spread through the house that I was getting *saaf* – pleading with the fridge instead of *baxing* her like a real Jamaican man should when things are *out of order* – then, the next thing you know, they'd start spreading rumours, like, "I hear Geoffrey begging the fridge to work. Imagine that. I always knew he was *saaf*." That would mean I'd have to start *baxing* the TV, stereo, and clothes-dryer – probably *mash up* a few to keep order in my house.

But like Brother Bob said, "We don't need no more trouble."

I patted her handle and asked her, "What's wrong, Luscious?"

She sputtered for a few moments.

"You better have a long talk with your son."

"Why?"

She remained quiet until the commercial break. Oprah was talking about a new, sensational diet.

"Two days ago," she said, "while you were upstairs on the computer (you wouldn't believe the things he says about you when you're not here – telling everybody and their mother which web sites you visit and how much money you *don't* have in the bank), your son just came down to the kitchen and tore open my two doors and kept looking at me like he lost something. Then, he had the nerve to leave me open all night. And you have the nerve to ask me what's wrong?"

"I will talk to the boy."

"You see, that's the first part of the problem. He is not a boy any more. He is a man! Ever since he started growing hair on his chest and over his lip, he feels he can just come here, tear me open, and treat me any way he wants to."

"You right, Luscious. You right," I said. "I will have him apologize to you."

"You better do something and do it fast. For that is a man you're dealing with."

I really didn't want to *chuck badness* on my half-Jamaican son who was now becoming a half-Jamaican man. I never have. I waited for him to come home from school.

As soon as he skateboarded up the driveway with his girlfriend, I called out to him, "*Bwai,* come here."

From the sound of my voice, he knew he was in trouble. But he figured I wouldn't embarrass him with his little girlfriend by his side.

"Yes, Dad?"

He was beginning to sound the way that Kamau Brathwaite described George Lamming as having an "organ voice".

"Come over here and apologize to the fridge."

He was surprised. This is one of my idiosyncrasies that we hide from outsiders and especially Americans, who if they found out would certainly report me to the police. Then all my neighbours might see me doing the "perp walk" because I'd been arrested for "reckless endangerment of a minor". And just for talking to a fridge. If they only knew what I was going to do to that *mout-amassi* computer!

"Dad, please don't do this in front of my friend."

He didn't realize how desperate I'd become. But my mother-in-law was coming over in two hours. And as President Bush kept telling us, "Desperate times calls for disparate measures."

"You know what you did," I said. "Now apologize."

He was going to disobey me, but he heard the tone in my voice. He also knew I was capable of *chucking badness*, so he walked over to the fridge and mumbled an apology.

"Talk louder," I said. "She can't hear you."

"I'm sorry," he said.

His American girlfriend, usually dressed in black and with

160

black eyeliner, lipstick and nail polish – Goths, they call them – turned to him and said, "You talk to your refrigerator? Neat!"

She then pulled out her brand new i-Phone and called her mother to complain. She asked her mother why they didn't have a fridge she could talk to. Her mother started crying and said if her father had paid the child support and hadn't run off with that little tramp from the office, then everything would have been all right. But she said she would try to get a talking fridge as soon as she could. But right now, her life was falling apart and she needed to take some Xanax before she went to see her therapist.

The little girl and her mother were having their own challenges, and more than I could handle. I turned to my son.

"Say it one more time," I said.

"I'm sorry, okay?"

Luscious purred back to life and my son went downstairs with his girlfriend. I would soon have to have that other talk with him.

But, in the meantime, I had more pressing concerns. I went to work stuffing the fridge with popsicles, beer, and sodas. By the time my mother in law came over at seven o'clock, everything was *cris' and curry*. I even got my mother-in-law to try a drink she'd resisted for as long as I've known her. I fixed her a cold *Ting* with crushed ice and that well-known corrupter of youth, Appleton Rum.

She looked at the drink, smelled it, but then saw the beads of water running down the side of the glass, and she took a sip.

"It's nice," she said and drank it all in one gulp. "*Mix up* another one."

My wife turned quickly and laughed. I laughed too.

"What? What?" asked my mother-in-law.

We didn't answer. Like I said, we've been married for more than twenty years. We know what's good for us.

ABOUT THE AUTHOR

Geoffrey Philp writes:
'I was born in Kingston, Jamaica, and I attended Mona Primary and Jamaica College, where I studied literature under the tutelage of Dennis Scott. When I left Jamaica in 1979, I went to Miami Dade College and after graduating, I studied Caribbean, African and African-American literature with Dr. O.R. Dathorne and creative writing with Lester Goran, Evelyn Wilde Mayerson, and Isaac Bashevis Singer. Since then, I have attended workshops with Derek Walcott, Edward Albee, and Israeli playwright, Matti Meged. As a James Michener Fellow at the University of Miami, I studied poetry under Kamau Brathwaite and fiction with George Lamming.

In 1990, I published my first book of poems, *Exodus and Other Poems,* and four other poetry collections have followed: *Florida Bound (1985), hurricane center (1998), xango music (2001),* and *Twelve Poems and A Story for Christmas (2005).* I have also written a book of short stories, *Uncle Obadiah and the Alien (1997),* and a novel, *Benjamin, My Son (2003)* which was set in Jamaica during the turbulent eighties – a time of gang and class warfare, mass exodus, and the emergence of reggae, Rastafari and Bob Marley.

I continue to work on many projects such as a children's book, *Grandpa Sydney's Anancy Stories,* and just completed a book of short stories, *Who's Your Daddy? and Other Stories* (Peepal Tree Press, 2009), a hypertext novel, *Virtual Yardies,* and a novel, *Miami Lovesong,* which is set in South Florida. The major stars of the novel are a hurricane, a missing daughter, and a Rastaman– kind of Zora Neale Hurston meets South Florida and Jamaica.

My poems and short stories have appeared in *Small Axe, Asili, The Caribbean Writer, Gulf Stream, Florida in Poetry: A History of the Imagination, Wheel and Come Again: An Anthology of Reggae Poetry, Whispers from the Cotton Tree Root, The Oxford Book of Caribbean Short Stories,* and *The Oxford Book of Caribbean Verse.*'

Geoffrey Philp has a popular Caribbean blogspot:
http://geoffreyphilp.blogspot.com

FICTION

Uncle Obadiah and the Alien
ISBN: 9781900715010; pp. 160; pub. 1997; £7.99

How does an alien with an unfortunate resemblance to Margaret Thatcher come to be in Uncle Obadiah's yard smoking all his best weed? This beautifully crafted and frequently hilarious collection of short stories is guaranteed to lift even the deepest gloom. Written in Jamaican patois and standard English, this is a brilliant read which will lead you through the yards of Jamaica to the streets of Miami. Here is a contemporary world, warts and all. Geoffrey Philp goes beyond stereotypes to portray the individuality and humanity in all his characters. And of course there is always the best lamb's breath colly to help improve the day.

Robert Antoni writes: 'If Dickens were reincarnated as a Jamaican Rastaman, he would write stories as hilarious and humane as these. "Uncle Obadiah" and the other stories collected here announce Geoffrey Philp as a direct descendent of Bob Marley: poet, philosophizer, spokesperson for our next new world.'

John Dufresne writes: 'Geoffrey Philp is a literary shaman, an enchanter, a weaver of spells that reveal unexpected and marvelous things about life, that carry the news of island culture to the mainland. From the first word of the first story in this comic and touching collection, Philp lifts me out of my world and drops me into the world of his charming, beleaguered and compelling characters. *Uncle Obadiah and the Alien* is one of those rare treasures, a book you can't put down and won't ever forget.'

Norval Edwards writes: 'Geoffrey Philp's writing combines a poetic sensibility with finely honed narrative skills that draw on a multitude of resources: literary and oral traditions, rasta and ragamuffin flavours, science fiction and Jamaican tall tales. Philp blends them all with humour, wisdom and craft.'

Benjamin, My Son
ISBN: 9781900715782; pp. 186; pub. 2003; £8.99

Jason Lumley is in a Miami bar when he sees a newsflash reporting the murder of his politician father, Albert Lumley. With his girlfriend, Nicole, Jason returns to his native Jamaica for the funeral. There the murder is regarded by all as part of the bipartisan warfare which has torn the country apart.

But when Jason meets his old mentor, Papa Legba, the Rastafarian hints at a darker truth. Under the guidance of his locksman Virgil, and redeemed by his love for the Beatrice-like figure of Nicole, Jason enters the several circles of Jamaica's hell. The portrayal of the garrison ghetto area of Standpipe is, in particular, profoundly disturbing.

In his infernal journeyings, Jason encounters both former acquaintances and earlier versions of himself. In the process he confronts conflicting claims on his identity: the Jason shaped by the middle-class colonial traditions of Jamaica College and the Benjamin who was once close to Papa Legba.

Benjamin, My Son combines the excitement of the fast-paced thriller, the literary satisfactions of its intertextual play and the bracing commentary of its portrayal of the sexism, homophobia and moral corruption which have filled the vacuum vacated by the collapse of the nationalist dream.

POETRY

Florida Bound
ISBN: 9780948833823; pp. 64; pub. 1995; £7.99

Geoffrey Philp was born and grew up in Jamaica. He now lives in Miami. His poems of exasperation and longing explore a reluctance to leave Jamaica and the 'marl-white roads at Struie' and anger that 'blackman still can't live in him own/black land' where 'gunman crawl like bedbug'. But whilst poems explore the keeness and sorrows of an exile's memory, the new landscape of South Florida landscape fully engages the poet's imagination. The experience of journeying is seen as part of a larger pattern of restless but creative movement in the Americas. Philp joins other Caribbean poets in making use of nation language, but few have pushed the collision between roots language and classical forms to greater effect.

Carrol Fleming writes in *The Caribbean Writer*: 'His poems are as vibrant and diverse as Miami where "each street crackles with dialects/variegated as the garish crotons". Miami, albeit citified, becomes just one more island with all that is good, bad and potentially violent beset by the same sea, same hurricanes, and "mangroves lashed sapless by the wind".

"Philp's poems wander through bedrooms and along the waterfronts of that perceptive land accessible only to poets, only to those who can pull the day through dawn fog to the delicate "breath of extinguished candles".

Hurricane Center
ISBN: 9781900715232; pp. 67; pub. 1998; £7.99

El nino stirs clouds over the Pacific. Flashing TV screens urge a calm that no one believes. The police beat a slouched body, crumpled like a fist of kleenex. The news racks are crowded with stories of pestilence, war and rumours of war. The children, once sepia-faced cherubim, mutate to monsters that eat, eat, eat. You notice a change in your body's conversation with itself, and in the garden the fire ants burrow into the flesh of the fruit.

Geoffrey Philps's poems stare into the dark heart of a world where hurricanes, both meteorological and metaphorical, threaten you to the last cell. But the sense of dread also reveals what is most precious in life, for the dark and accidental are put in the larger context of season and human renewal, and *Hurricane Center* returns always to the possibilities of redemption and joy.

In the voices of Jamaican prophets, Cuban exiles, exotic dancers, drunks, race-track punters, canecutters, rastamen, middle-class householders and screw-face ghetto sufferers, Geoffrey Philp writes poetry which is both intimately human and cosmic in scale. On the airwaves between Miami and Kingston, the rhythms of reggae and mambo dance through these poems.

Xango Music

ISBN: 9781900715461; pp. 64; pub. 2001; £7.99

In the Xango ceremony, the contraries of New World African experience find transcendence. From the established, bodily patterns of ritual comes release into the freedom of the spirit; from the exposure of pain comes the possibilities of healing; and for the individual there is both the dread aloneness with the gods and the 'we-ness' of community.

Simultaneously the rites celebrate the rich, syncretic diversity, the multiple connections of the African person in the New World and enact the tragic search for the wholeness of the lost African centre. And there is the god himself, standing at the crossroads, 'beating iron into the shape of thunder', both the prophetic voice warning of the fire to command the creator who hammers out sweet sound from the iron drum.

Geoffrey Philp finds in Xango a powerful metaphor that is both particular to the Caribbean and universal in its relevance.

David and Phyllis Gershator writes in *The Caribbean Writer*: 'Using rhythm and riffs, he can pull the stops on language and give it a high energy kick. In 'jam-rock' he winds up with 'the crack of bones, the sweat of the whip; girl, you gonna get a lot of it; get it galore; my heart still beats uncha, uncha uncha, cha'.

All Peepal Tree titles are available from the website
www.peepaltreepress.com
with a money back guarantee, secure credit card ordering
and fast delivery throughout the world at cost or less.

Peepal Tree Press is celebrated as the home of challenging and inspiring literature from the Caribbean and Black Britain. Visit www.peepaltreepress.com to read sample poems and reviews, discover new authors, established names and access a wealth of information. Subscribe to our mailing list for news of new books and events.

Contact us at:
Peepal Tree Press, 17 King's Avenue, Leeds LS6 1QS, UK
Tel: +44 (0) 113 2451703 E-mail: contact@peepaltreepress.com